¿Habla Español?

To Detlef, for laughing with me everyday.

Published in the United States by Living Language, a Random House Company

www.livinglanguage.com

Editor: Chris Warnasch
Production Editor: John Whitman
Production Managers: Helen Kilcullen and Heather Lanigan
Interior Design: Sophie Ye Chin

First Edition

ISBN 1-4000-2092-1

Library of Congress Cataloging-in-Publication Data available upon request.

This book is available for special discounts for bulk purchases for sales promotions or premiums. Special editions, including personalized covers, excerpts of existing books, and corporate imprints, can be created in large quantities for special needs. For more information, write to Special Markets/Premium Sales, 1745 Broadway, MD 6-2, New York, New York 10019 or e-mail specialmarkets@randomhouse.com.

PRINTED IN THE UNITED STATES OF AMERICA

10 9 8 7 6 5 4 3 2 1

¿Habla Español?

LEARN SPANISH

The Basics

by

Enrique Montes

edited by

Christopher A. Warnasch

STANDARD DEVIANTS

Table of Contents

Introduction

Welcome to *¿Habla Español? Learn Spanish: The Basics,* an exciting and entertaining new way to learn Spanish, brought to you by LIVING LANGUAGE and THE STANDARD DEVIANTS.

This is the right course for you if A) you've always wanted to learn Spanish, B) you've never had the time, and C) you've been bored to tears or scared senseless by more traditional courses. The experts at Living Language and The Standard Deviants have gotten together to bring you something truly unique – a course that's fun and entertaining, complete with a perfectly coordinated book and DVD that really, honestly work. This is the perfect way to learn Spanish for anyone who wants to have a good time along with all the learning. Maybe you're going on a trip to Madrid or Mexico City, or you want to impress someone special, or you want to get ahead on the job, or you're just looking for some personal enrichment. Or maybe you're taking an introductory Spanish course but need a little extra inspiration to make sense of it all. In any of those cases, this is a great course for you.

Here's how it works. The package includes a 192-page book and a DVD, each of which is the perfect companion to the other. The book and the DVD work together to teach and reinforce, and to give you plenty of opportunity to learn, practice, and review. They're simple to use. The course has three parts, and each of those parts is divided into a few sections. All you have to do is read a section in the book, complete with explanations, examples, vocabulary and practice exercises. Then, once you've finished digesting the information, watch the corresponding section on the DVD. You'll find more explanations, more examples, and even more practice exercises. And last, for good measure, turn back to the book and do the review exercises. Simple! Here goes again:

1. Start with the book. Read the section, learn the vocabulary, and do the practice exercises.
2. Watch the corresponding section on the DVD. Choose "Select Lesson" from the main menu.
3. Turn back to the book. Do the Review Exercises at the end of the section to wrap it all up.

This course covers all of the basics of Spanish. You'll learn pronunciation, greetings and basic vocabulary, how to talk a little bit about yourself and ask about others, and you'll get a good taste of grammar. This is the perfect way to start learning Spanish – you'll get a solid foundation in what you absolutely need to know, and best of all, you'll actually *enjoy* doing it, so you'll be all set to continue your studies! Great, right?

Ready? Let's begin!

How to use
the DVD

1 Place the **DVD** disk into the player. After a brief intro, the main menu will appear on the screen.

2 Use the **UP** and **DOWN** arrows to move among the menu choices. Press **ENTER** to select.

3 During the program, press **MENU** to return to the main menu. Access special features, including **HELPFUL INFO** and the **FINAL EXAM** from the main menu.

4 During the program, press the **NEXT** and **PREV** buttons to skip through major sections of the program.

¿Habla Español?

Oh, Yeah,
You Can Speak Spanish!

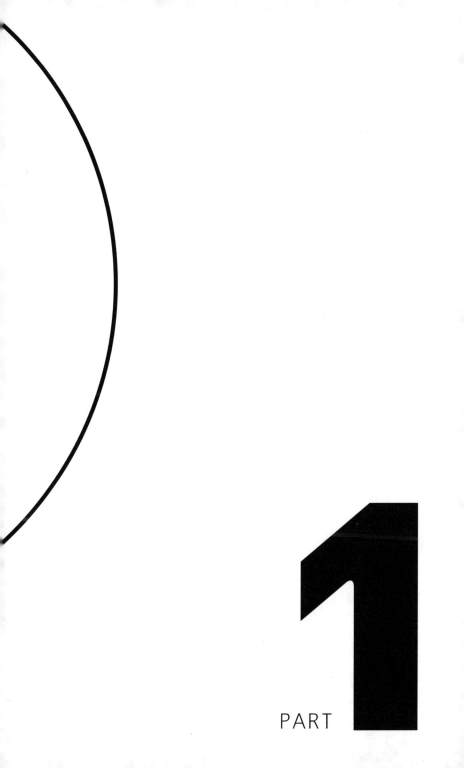

PART 1

Before We Get Started . . .

Before you start to speak Spanish, it might be helpful to remember where Spanish comes from. Remember Latin? Ot-nay Ig-Pay Atin-Lay, but the real McKoy. Latin was the language of Rome, and from Latin came today's Romance Languages. And by Romance Languages we don't mean The Languages of Love (at least not necessarily, but that's up to you . . .). The term Romance comes from the word Rome, and the Romance Languages include Spanish, French, Italian, Portuguese, Romanian, and a few others.

Spanish is spoken by over 300,000,000 people across the world. It's the official language not just of Spain (*España*), of course, but also of most of Latin America: *México, Honduras, Guatemala, El Salvador, Costa Rica, Nicaragua, Panamá, Puerto Rico, Cuba*, the Domincan Republic (*la República Dominicana*), *Venezuela, Colombia, Perú, Ecuador, Chile, Bolivia, Argentina, Paraguay, Uruguay* . . .

That's a lot of people in a lot of different places. So, you'll be in good company as a Spanish speaker. Ready to get started? *¡Muy bien! ¡Vámonos!* (Very Good! Let's go!) Turn back to your DVD and watch the first section.

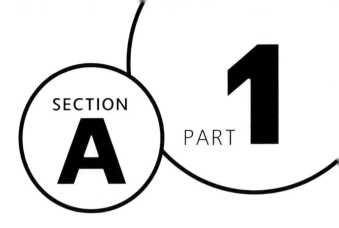

SECTION **A** PART **1**

Pronunciation

Now let's get started on the alphabet and pronunciation. In every section of this course, you'll first get some words to add to your vocabulary. You'll hear these words used in examples throughout the section, and since you're learning a language, which is of course made up of words, you should try to make them stick eventually. But that doesn't mean you have to memorize every single word right away. Just get a good sense of them so that you'll recognize them when you see them used later on in the section.

POINT 1: VOCABULARY

TIPS FOR MEMORIZING VOCABULARY: Some vocabulary is going to look the same as, or at least a lot like, its English counterpart. You can guess what these words mean: *patio, electricidad, humana, idiota* . . . They're called cognates, and they're the easiest vocabulary words to remember.

But what if a word isn't a cognate? Well, there are tricks for them, too.

▶ Repetition works well. Write a word, and say it aloud, several times.
▶ Flash cards are a good trick, too. Write the Spanish on one side, and the English on the other. Then quiz yourself.
▶ Mnemonics, or memory tricks, are also a great way to memorize vocabulary (or anything else, for that matter.) For example, *eructo* means burp. *Eructo* sounds like "erupt," which is what you might imagine if you hear a big, long, loud . . . Well, maybe we should try something less gross. Like, *ciudad* (see-yoo-DAHD), which means "city." You could imagine yourself walking out the door, saying "See you, Dad! I'm going to the city for the day."

Okay, as promised, here are those words you should be able to recognize! And, since you don't quite know how to pronounce them yet, you'll see [fuh-NEH-tikz] to give you a boost in the beginning. Remember that they're not perfect, but they'll be a big help and a close approximation at least.

cena [SEH-nah] – dinner
eructo [eh-ROOK-toh] – burp
pelo [PEH-loh] – hair

muy [MWEE] – very

bonito [boh-NEE-toh] – pretty

cine [SEE-neh] – movies, cinema

idiota [ee-DYOH-tah] – idiot

ojo [OH-hoh] – eye

ojo morado [OH-hoh moh-RAH-doh] – black eye

trucha [TROO-chah] trout

estúpida [eh-STOO-pee-dah] – stupid

consonante [kohn-soh-NAHN-teh]– consonant

buena [BWEH-nah] – good

vaca [BAH-kah] – cow

ciudad [see-yoo-DAHD] – city

curso [KOOR-soh] – course

calle [KAH-yeh] – street

coche [KOH-cheh] – car

carro [KAH-rroh] – car

gracias [GRAH-syahs] – thank you

gato [GAH-toh] – cat

regalo [reh-GAH-loh] – present

general [heh-neh-RAHL] – general

magia [MAH-hee-yah] – magic

inteligente [een-teh-lee-HEHN-teh] – smart, intelligent

guante [GWAHN-teh] – glove

garaje [gah-RAH-heh] – garage

gordo [GOHR-doh] – fat

guerra [GEH-rrah] – war

guitarra [ghee-TAH-rrah] – guitar

pingüino [peen-GWEE-noh] – penguin

cigüeña [see-GWEH-nyah] – stork

hormiga [ohr-MEE-gah]– ant

huevo [WEH-boh] – egg

ahora [ah-OH-rah]– now

juntos [HOON-tohs]– together

naranja [nah-RAHN-hah]– orange

joven [HOH-vehn]– young

bolsa [BOHL-sah] – purse, bag

llave [YAH-beh] – key

amarillo [ah-mah-REE-yoh]– yellow

año [AH-nyoh] – year

niño [NEE-nyoh] – boy

uña [OOH-nyah] – fingernail

quinto [KEEN-toh] – fifth

queso [KEH-soh] – cheese

querido [keh-REE-doh] – dear, beloved

ferrocarril [feh-rroh-kah-REEL] – railway, train

rápido [RAH-pee-doh] – quick, fast, rapid

zapato [sah-PAH-toh] – shoe

azúcar [ah-SOO-kahr] – sugar

tetera [teh-TEH-rah] – teapot

no más [noh MAHS] – no more

cocos [KOH-kohs] – coconuts

justicia humana [hoo-STEE-syah oo-MAH-nah] – human justice

aguacate [ah-wah-KAH-teh] – avocado

guacamole [gwah-kah-MOH-leh] – guacamole

siete [SYEH-teh] – seven

PRACTICE EXERCISE 1

Match each of the Spanish words in the left column with the English meaning in the right column.

1.	*tetera*	car
2.	*coche*	yellow
3.	*guitarra*	orange
4.	*amarillo*	eye
5.	*joven*	now
6.	*cena*	train
7.	*ojo*	teapot
8.	*naranja*	guitar
9.	*cigüeña*	dinner
10.	*ahora*	stork
11.	*ferrocarril*	young

PRACTICE EXERCISE 2

Fill in the blanks for each of the Spanish words below.

1. Coconuts are *c__ co __*.
2. A *pi__ gü __ __ o* is a penguin.
3. If something is fast, it's *r __ pi __ __*.
4. If you want to put your car in a garage, you put it in a *__ __ ra __ __*.
5. Those little black insects that spoil your picnic are *ho __ __ ig __ s*.
6. Hair is *__ __ l __*.
7. A cat, or a *__ __ __ __ __*, could make a great present,
   or a *r __ __ a __ o*.
8. Both the fruit and the color are called *n __ r __ n __ __*.
9. Between fourth and sixth is *q __ i __ __ o*.
10. Don't wait until later, do it *a __ o __ __*!

There are twenty-seven letters in the Spanish alphabet. They've got all of the letters in the English alphabet, plus ñ. That's called "en-yay," like the singer but with a "yayl" at the end. The little squiggle over the top of the n is called a *tilde* [TEEL-deh].

A, B, C, D, E, F, G, H, I, J, K, L, M, N, Ñ, O, P, Q, R, S, T, U, V, W, X, Y, Z

These are the names of the letters:

a, be, ce, de, e, efe, ge, hache, i, jota, ka, ele, eme, ene, eñe, o, pe, cu, ere, ese, te, u, ve, doble ve, equis, i-griega, zeta

Or, if you want to see them in phonetics, that would be:

[AH, BEH, SEH, DEH, EH, EH-feh, HEH, AH-cheh, EE, HOH-tah, KAH, EH-leh, EH-meh, EH-neh, EH-nyeh, OH, PEH, KOO, EH-reh, EH-seh, TEH, OOH, BEH, DOH-bleh BEH, EH-kees, ee-gree-YEH-gah, SEH-tah]

Since we're talking about letters, we should add that there used to be two other letters in the Spanish alphabet. *Ch* and *ll* were up until recently considered their own separate letters. *Ch* was called "cheh," like the guy on all the tee-shirts, with a pronunciation just like the English ch – ch as in *church*. The double l was called "eh-yay" with a pronunciation like the English y as in *yes*. These spellings still exist in Spanish – you'll see an awful lot of them in fact. But now they're not considered their own letters.

POINT 3: VOWELS

There are just five vowels in Spanish: *a, e, i, o, u.* They have short, crisp, pure sounds: ah, eh, ee, oh, oo. Remember not to drag them out the way we do in English. (You know – "say" is pronounced like seh-ee and "boat" is pronounced like boh-woot.) They should be nice and clean: ah, eh, ee, oh, oo.

a: *María* [mah-REE-yah]

e: *la cena* [lah SEH-nah]
      el eructo [ehl eh-ROOK-toh]

i: *el cine* [ehl SEE-neh]
      una idiota [OO-nah ee-DYOH-tah]

o: *un ojo* [oon OH-hoh]
      un ojo morado [oon OH-hoh moh-RAH-doh]

u: *una trucha* [OO-nah TROO-chah]
      una trucha estúpida [OO-nah TROO-chah eh-STOO-pee-dah]
      un eructo [oon eh-ROOK-toh]

POINT 4: CONSONANTS

Many consonants in Spanish are pronounced pretty much like we pronounce them in English. But there are just 10 rules that you should remember to tackle the ones that are a bit different.

RULE 1 B and V are both pronounced like a soft B, at least in most Spanish-speaking countries.

venir, buena, vaca, burro

[beh-NEER, BWEH-nah, BAH-kah, BOO-roh]

RULE 2 C before E or I is pronounced like an S.

cena, cine, ciudad

[SEH-nah, SEE-neh, see-yoo-DAHD]

But in Spain, a C before E or I is pronounced like a TH. It's not a lisp – it's the way it's really pronounced!

cena, cine, ciudad

[THEH-nah, THEE-neh, thee-yoo-DAHD]

And, a C before A, O, or U is pronounced like a hard K.

curso, calle, coche

[KOOR-soh, KAH-yeh, KOH-cheh]

RULE 3 G before a consonant, A, O, or U is pronounced like a hard G.

gracias, gato, regalo, guante, gordo

[GRAH-syahs, GAH-toh, reh-GAH-loh, GWAHN-teh, GOHR-doh]

But a G before I or E is pronounced almost like an H.

general, magia, inteligente

[heh-neh-RAHL, MAH-hee-yah, een-teh-lee-HEHN-teh]

To make a hard G before an I or E, the spelling GUE or GUI is used.

guerra, guitarra

[GEH-rah, ghee-TAH-rah]

But if there are two dots (a dieresis) over that U, as in ÜE or ÜI, the U is pronounced a lot like a W.

pingüino, cigüeña

[peen-GWEE-noh, see-GWEH-nyah]

RULE **4** **The H is silent.**

hormiga, huevo

[ohr-MEE-gah, WEH-boh]

RULE **5** **J is pronounced almost like an H.**

juntos, naranja, joven

[HOON-tohs, nah-RAHN-hah, HOH-behn]

RULE **6** **LL is pronounced like a Y.**

Ella lleva la llave en una bolsa amarilla. (She carries the key in a yellow purse.)

[EH-yah YEH-bah lah YAH-beh ehn OO-nah BOHL-sah ah-mah-REE-yah]

RULE **7** **Ñ is pronounced like ny, the sound in "canyon" or "onion." And don't forget that the squiggle is called a *tilde*.**

año, niño, uña

[AH-nyoh, NEE-nyoh, OO-nyah]

RULE **8** **Q is pronounced like a K, and it's always written before a UI or a UE. Notice that the U is not pronounced!**

Mi quinto queso querido . . . (My fifth beloved cheese . . .)

[mee KEEN-toh KEH-soh keh-REE-doh]

RR is pronounced with a long role or a trill. It takes practice!

carro, burro

[KAH-rroh, BOO-rroh]

El carro y el ferrocarril corren rápido. (The car and the train go fast.)

[ehl KAH-roh ee ehl feh-roh-kah-REEL KOH-rehn RAH-pee-doh]

Also notice that an R at the beginning of a word is pronounced the same way.

Rubén riñe con una rata en Río. (Ruben quarrels with a rat in Rio.)

[roo-BEHN REE-nyeh kohn OO-nah RAH-tah ehn REE-yoh]

Z is pronounced like an S in Latin America, but like a TH in Spain.

El zapato de Zorro está en el azúcar. (Zorro's shoe is in the sugar.)

[ehl sah-PAH-toh deh SOH-roh ehs-TAH ehn ehl ah-SOO-kahr] in Latin America.

[ehl thah-PAH-toh deh THOH-roh ehs-TAH ehn ehl ah-THOO-kahr] in Spain.

And remember that our English Z sound (zip, zap, zipper) does not exist in Spanish.

PRACTICE EXERCISE 3

Answer each of the following questions. *¡Buena suerte!* Good Luck!

1. Which one of these words has a "y" as in "yes" sound in it?: *PELO, LLEVA, UÑA*
2. Which of these words has a hard "k" sound in it? *CENA, CIGÜEÑA, COCHE*
3. Which of these words has a hard "g" sound in it? *GATO, GENERAL, MAGIA*
4. Which one of these English words starts with a sound similar to the way a J in Spanish sounds? JELLY, ZIPPER, HAPPY
5. What other Spanish letter is pronounced like a Spanish B?
6. What letter do you always see with a Q in Spanish?
7. The sound of the double RR is a long role or trill. When is the single letter R pronounced the same way?
8. What is the sound of the letter Z is Latin America?
9. What is the sound of the letter Z in Spain?
10. What is the sound of LL as in *amarillo*?

PRACTICE EXERCISE 4

Try to say these sentences aloud to yourself. Don't worry – you'll hear them again and have a chance to repeat when you watch the DVD. But give it a shot on your own, first.

1. *Mi mamá me ama.*
2. *Viviana visita la India.*
3. *Yo como cocos con Carlos.*
4. *Lucía lucha por la justicia humana.*

Did you catch the meaning of those sentences, by the way? In case you didn't:

1. My Mom loves me.
2. Viviana visits India.
3. I eat coconuts with Carlos.
4. Lucia fights for human justice.

POINT 5: DIPHTHONGS

A diphthong is a sound that's a combination of two vowels, but pronounced as one syllable. For example, the vowel in English say, bay, hey! is actually a diphthong of eh + ee. Try it yourself – say eh, ee, eh, ee, eh, ee really fast. Soon you're saying ay, ay, ay . . . In Spanish the diphthongs are a combination of the vowels A, E, I, O, and U.

IE sounds like a quick ee + eh, or "yeh"
EI sounds like eh + ee, or something close to our English –ay in bay or say.
IA sounds like a quick ee + ah, or "yah"
IO sounds like a quick ee + oh, or "yoh"
IU sounds like a quick ee + oo, or "yoo"
EA sounds like a quick eh +ah
EU sounds like a quick eh+oo
UE sounds like a quick oo + eh, or something close to "weh"
UA sounds like a quick oo + ah, or something close to "wah"
UI sounds like a quick oo + ee, or something like "wee"
AU sounds like a quick ah + oo, similar to the sound in "ouch" or "brown"

And so on . . . just pronounce both sounds together quickly, as one syllable.

PRACTICE EXERCISE 5

Try pronouncing these words. Watch out for the diphthongs!

aguacate (avocado), *siete* (seven), *seis* (six), *Santiago* (the city), *pueblo* (village), *puedo* (can, as in "able to"), *neutro* (neutral), *patio* (patio), *cuidado* (carefull)

(NOW, WATCH THE DVD)

If you've digested this information, turn on your DVD, choose "Select Lesson," and watch Section 2. Then don't forget to come back to the book, though, for some final review . . .

REVIEW EXERCISES

Now that you've gone through the section in the book, and then watched it on the DVD, here's a chance to show what you know.

REVIEW EXERCISE 1

Give the Spanish translation of each of the following words.

1. present
2. pretty
3. city
4. garage
5. railway
6. seven

7. egg
8. yellow
9. fat
10. cheese

REVIEW EXERCISE 2

Say whether the following statements are TRUE or FALSE

1. T F The letters B and V have the same pronunciation in most Spanish-speaking countries.
2. T F In Spain, the letter C before an E or I is pronounced like a TH.
3. T F In Latin America, the letter C before an E or I is pronounced like an S.
4. T F The letter G before a consonant is pronounced like a J.
5. T F The letter H in Spanish is silent.
6. T F The sound of the double LL is the same as the sound of L.
7. T F The sound of Ñ is the similar to the sound of NY.
8. T F The letter G has a hard sound in GUE and GUI.
9. T F The letter C before an A, O or U is pronounced like an S.
10. T F The English sound of Z doesn't exist in Spanish.

REVIEW EXERCISE 3

Complete the following sentences.

1. You use shampoo to wash your __ e __ o.
2. He gets very high grades, he's very __ n __ __ l __ g __ n __ __.
3. "Moo" said the v __ c __.
4. War and Peace in Spanish is "G __ e __ r __ y Paz."
5. It's not a vowel, it's a __ o __ s __ n __ n __ __.

6. Nueva York is an example of a __ i __ d __ __.
7. The three meals are breakfast, lunch and __ e __ a.
8. The opposite of old is j __ v __ n.
9. He plays the piano but he's not good at playing the __ u __ t __ rr __.
10. For her birthday she received a good __ e __ a __ o.

REVIEW EXERCISE 4

The following is a list of countries where Spanish is an official language. Fill in the blanks below.

1. A __ g __ n __ i __ a
2. B __ l __ v __ a
3. C __ i __ e
4. C __ l __ m __ i __
5. C __ s __ a R __ c __
6. C __ b __
7. E __ u __ d __ r
8. E __ S __ l __ a __ o __
9. E __ p __ ñ __
10. G __ a __ e __ a __ a
11. H __ n __ u __ a __
12. M __ x __ c __
13. N __ c __ r __ g __ a
14. P __ n __ m __
15. P __ r __ g __ a __
16. P __ r __
17. P __ e __ t __ R __ c __
18. R __ p __ b __ i __ a D __ m __ n __ c __ n __
19. U __ u __ u __ y
20. V __ n __ z __ e __ a

Answer Key

PRACTICE EXERCISE 1

1. *tetera* – teapot
2. *coche* – car
3. *guitarra* – guitar
4. *amarillo* – yellow
5. *joven* – young
6. *cena* – dinner
7. *ojo* – eye
8. *naranja* – orange
9. *cigüeña* – stork
10. *ahora* – now
11. *ferrocarril* – train

PRACTICE EXERCISE 2

1. Coconuts are cocos.
2. A pingüino is a penguin.
3. If something is fast, it's rápido.
4. If you want to put your car in a garage, you put it in a garaje.
5. Those little black insects that spoil your picnic are hormigas.
6. Hair is pelo.
7. A cat, or a gato, could make a great present, or a regalo.
8. Both the fruit and the color are called naranja.
9. Between fourth and sixth is quinto.
10. Don't wait until later, do it ahora!

PRACTICE EXERCISE 3

1. LLEVA
2. COCHE
3. GATO
4. HAPPY
5. V
6. U
7. At the beginning of a word
8. It's the S sound
9. It's the TH sound
10. It's the Y sound

REVIEW EXERCISE 1

1. present – regalo
2. pretty – bonito
3. city – ciudad
4. garage – garaje
5. railway – ferrocarril

6. seven – siete

7. egg – huevo

8. yellow – amarillo

9. fat – gordo

10. cheese – queso

REVIEW EXERCISE 2

1. TRUE

2. TRUE

3. TRUE

4. FALSE

5. TRUE

6. FALSE

7. TRUE

8. TRUE

9. FALSE

10. TRUE

REVIEW EXERCISE 3

1. You use shampoo to wash your pelo.

2. He gets very high grades, he's very inteligente.

3. "Moo" said the vaca.

4. War and Peace in Spanish is *"Guerra y Paz."*

5. It's not a vowel, it's a consonante.

6. Nueva York is an example of a ciudad.

7. The three meals are breakfast, lunch and cena.

8. The opposite of old is joven.

9. He plays the piano but he's not good at playing the guitarra.

10. For her birthday she received a good regalo.

REVIEW EXERCISE 4

1. Argentina
2. Bolivia
3. Chile
4. Colombia
5. Costa Rica
6. Cuba
7. Ecuador
8. El Salvador
9. España
10. Guatemala
11. Honduras
12. México
13. Nicaragua
14. Panamá
15. Paraguay
16. Perú
17. Puerto Rico
18. República Dominicana
19. Uruguay
20. Venezuela

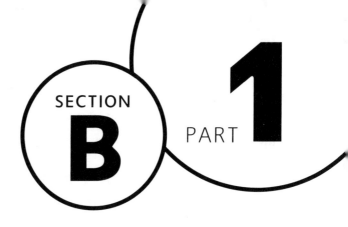

Capitalization and Accents

In this section we're going to learn about capitalization and accent marks. Accent marks are those annoying little marks that are sometimes placed above Spanish vowels. They happen to be very important because not only do they change the stress of the syllable, but sometimes they can even change the meaning of a word. When writing a word that has an accent mark, don't leave it out! Let's see why . . . If you generally have bad table manners and you want to ask someone how you are eating, you would ask the person: ¿*Cómo como*? (How am I eating?). Notice that the word ¿*Cómo*? has an accent mark and it means "how?" whereas the word *como* doesn't have an accent mark and it means "I eat" or "I am eating." We'll come back to all of that in just a bit.

Remember what your elementary school teacher told you about English capitalization? Well, now that you remember, you can forget about it. The Spanish language follows its own rules when it comes to capitalization, and in some cases the rules are the opposite of English!

Remember the meaning of *cena* and *vaca*? Good, because now we are ready to learn some new words. Let's concentrate on some new vocabulary that will be helpful in this section of the DVD.

POINT 1: VOCABULARY

modo [MOH-doh] – way or manner

americano [ah-meh-reh-KAH-noh] – American* (see note at end of list)

modo americano [MOH-doh ah-meh-ree-KAH-noh] – American way

café [kah-FEH] – coffee

colombiano [koh-lohm-BYAH-noh] – Colombian

loco [LOH-koh] – crazy, lunatic

presidente [preh-see-DEHN-teh] – president

nombre [NOHM-breh] – name

rosa [ROH-sah] – rose

sombrero [sohm-BREH-roh] – hat

nuevo [NWEH-boh] – new

té [TEH] – tea

tulipán [too-lee-PAHN] –tulip

clavel [KLAH-behl] – carnation

argentino [ahr-hehn-TEE-noh] – Argentinian

cubano [koo-BAH-noh] – Cuban

venezolano [beh-neh-soh-LAH-noh] – Venezuelan

hondureño [ohn-doo-REH-nyoh] – Honduran

costarricense [koh-stah-rree-SEHN-seh] – Costa Rican

dominicano [doh-mee-nee-KAH-noh] – Dominican

puertorriqueño [pwehr-toh-rree-KEH-nyoh] – Puerto Rican

chileno [chee-LEH-noh] – Chilean

peruano [pehr-WAH-noh] – Peruvian

mexicano [meh-hee-KAH-noh] – Mexican

*NOTE: The word *americano* means "American" in the sense of "from North or South America" or "from the Americas." A person from the United States of America isn't called *americano* by Latin Americans, but *estadounidense* [eh-stah-doh-oo-nee-DEHN-seh], which means "from the United States."

PRACTICE EXERCISE 1
Match the Spanish word in the left column with the English word in the right column.

1.	*loco*	new
2.	*rosa*	Cuban
3.	*yo*	coffee
4.	*nuevo*	carnation
5.	*café*	rose
6.	*clavel*	wonder
7.	*tulipán*	tea
8.	*costarricense*	crazy or lunatic
9.	*dominicano*	woman
10.	*peruano*	Costa Rican
11.	*cubano*	tulip
12.	*modo*	Dominican
13.	*mujer*	I
14.	*maravilla*	way
15.	*té*	Peruvian

PRACTICE EXERCISE 2
Fill in the blanks for each of the Spanish words below.

1. A person from Costa Rica is a __ o __ t __ r r __ c __ n __ e.
2. If you were born in the Dominican Republican, you are d __ m __ n __ c __ n __.

3. The guy who's acting crazy is very __ o __ o.
4. The American Way in Spanish is el __ o __ o a __ e __ __ c __ n __.
5. Most people drink a cup of hot c __ __ __ in the morning.
6. The man from Colombia is el hombre c __ l __ m __ i __ __ o.
7. Because of his nationality, Fidel Castro is __ u __ a __ __.
8. In England, drinking __ __ is more common than coffee.
9. When traveling in the Netherlands you are likely to encounter a t __ l __ p __ n.
10. The Spanish word for carnation is __ l __ v __ l.

POINT 2: RULES OF CAPITALIZATION

Many of the rules of capitalization that you learned as a child in school will no longer count. Just throw them out the windowl Let's go over the rules of Spanish capitalization. They may seem strange at first, but you'll get used to them in no time.

RULE **1** The names of the days of the week and the names of the months of the year are not capitalized in Spanish.

RULE **2** In Spanish, "I" means yo. In English we always capitalize the pronoun "I." Never capitalize the Spanish pronoun yo unless it's at the beginning of a sentence.

RULE **3** In Spanish, do not capitalize a proper adjective when it refers to a nationality. For example, in the English phrase "Colombian coffee" you need to capitalize the proper adjective Colombian. This is not the case in Spanish where the phrase translates as *café colombiano*. Now notice the English phrase "American way." Here, you also need to capitalize the proper adjective American. That is not the case in the Spanish equivalent *el modo americano*. (Also notice how the order of the adjective and noun is reversed . . . but more on that later.)

RULE **4** In Spanish, do not capitalize a proper noun, either, when it refers to a nationality. Proper nouns that refer to nationalities are capitalized in English. In the phrase "the lunatic American" you need to capitalize the word American. Do not do this in Spanish! The equivalent is *el americano loco*. This unfortunate condition not only happens to Americans, notice the expressions *el dominicano loco, el peruano loco, el cubano loco, el colombiano loco* and *el costarricense loco*.

RULE **5** This rule will be easy to remember because it is the same as in English. Names or parts of a name are always capitalized, even if they are proper adjectives. This applies to names of people, cities or countries. Notice the capitalization in these examples: *Roberto, Buenos Aires, México, la Mujer Maravilla* (Wonder Woman), *Estados Unidos de América* (United States of America). If it is a name or part of a name, CAPITALIZE IT!

RULE **6** Here is another easy rule. In Spanish, capital letters are always used at the beginning of sentences. Notice that the first word of the sentence is capitalized in: *El nuevo tulipán* *dominicano está loco.* You were right if you guessed that the sentence means "The new Dominican tulip is crazy." You're also right if you think that this sentence means nothing!

RULE **7** The names of titles are not capitalized in Spanish. In English you capitalize both words in "President Lincoln." In Spanish you would write *el presidente Lincoln.* Notice that you do not capitalize the title. You do, however, capitalize Lincoln because it is a proper name.

RULE **8** In Spanish you only capitalize the first word of the title of a book. In English you capitalize all the words of the title, except small words such as articles, conjunctions and prepositions. For example, in English there are three words that are capitalized in the book "The Name of the Rose." You capitalize the first word of the title, as well as the words Name and Rose, words that are considered important in the title. In Spanish you only capitalize the first word in the title. The Spanish equivalent of "The Name of the Rose" is *El nombre de la rosa.* Of course, if the title contains a proper name, you need to capitalize it as well. But you knew that! So "Curious George Buys a New Hat" is *Curious George compra un sombrero.* You always capitalize the first word, Curious, but in this case you need to capitalize George because it is a proper name.

PRACTICE EXERCISE 3

Say whether the following statements are True or False.

1. T F In Spanish, you always capitalize the first letter of the first word in a title of a book.
2. T F If there is a name of a country in the title of a book you need to capitalize it as well.
3. T F The capitalization in this sentence is correct: *La mujer Maravilla es muy bonita.*
4. T F The word *yo* means you.
5. T F The word *yo* is capitalized at the beginning of a sentence.
6. T F Names of days of the week are not capitalized unless they are at the beginning of a sentence.
7. T F People's titles are always capitalized.
8. T F If a sentence begins with the Spanish word for "I," the sentence is not capitalized.
9. T F A noun that refers to a person's nationality is not capitalized unless it is at the beginning of a sentence.
10. T F When writing the date in Spanish you capitalize only the month of the year.

PRACTICE EXERCISE 4

Underline the letter or letters that need to be capitalized in each sentence.

1. *"harry potter" es un libro de j. k. rowling.*
2. *yo soy una persona.*
3. *la persona soy yo.*
4. *el presidente lincoln es un presidente importante.*
5. *buenos aires, lima, caracas y santiago son ciudades de américa latina.*

6. *luisa es una señora colombiana.*
7. *hoy es lunes 13 de febrero.*
8. *"el nombre de la rosa" es un libro de umberto eco.*
9. *san juan es la capital de puerto rico.*
10. *la mujer maravilla no es la presidenta de los estados unidos de américa.*

POINT 3: ACCENTS

Have you noticed those pesky little marks above vowels in certain Spanish words? They are called accent marks and are very much an integral part of the structure of the word. Have you ever thought of simply eliminating them and not worrying about them? Well, forget about it! Eliminating accent marks would not only change the pronunciation of the word but it may change its meaning as well. This is why it is very important to consider accent marks as part of the spelling of the word. So resist the temptation, don't leave those accent marks out!

Accents are related to word stress. The rules of stress in Spanish (as in, why we say a SUSpect, but to susPECT in English) are a little complicated. Luckily, this isn't the time to study all of them; we'll just cover what you need to know right now.

What you need to know at this point is that every word in Spanish has one syllable that carries the most stress. An accent mark indicates when there is an irregularity in the pattern or rhythm of a word. For example, *tomo* [TOH-moh] means "I take" and the stress is on the first syllable, which is where it should be according to the normal, regular rules. But *tomó* [toh-MOH] means "took," and the stress is in the last syllable. That accent on the second *ó* means "forget the regular rules." In this example there is both a difference in pronunciation and meaning. Here is another example: The word *solo* [SOH-loh] means "alone" but *sólo* [SOH-loh] with an accent mark means "only." There's no change in pronunciation there. Another example like this is the word *se* [SEH], which is a reflexive pronoun and *sé* [SEH] with an accent mark, which means "I know."

Another easy thing to remember about accents is that question words in Spanish have accent marks. These are some of the most common question words in Spanish; notice how they all have accent marks:

¿qué? [KEH] – what?
¿cómo? [KOH-moh] – how?
¿por qué? [pohr KEH] – why?
¿cuándo? [KWAHN-doh] – when?
¿dónde? [DOHN-deh] – where?
¿quién? [KYEHN] – who?

Confused? Don't be. Here is a summary of what you need to know so far about accent marks. Accent marks:

▶ indicate that a word has an irregular stress pattern.
▶ may indicate that a word has two meanings. An accent mark differentiates one meaning from another.
▶ are used in question words at the beginning of a question.
▶ ought to be memorized as part of the spelling of the word. Do not leave them out!

PRACTICE EXERCISE 5

Match the Spanish question word in the left column with the English question word in the right column.

1. *¿cuándo?*   where?
2. *¿quién?*   why?
3. *¿dónde?*   what?
4. *¿qué?*   when?
5. *¿cómo?*   who?
6. *¿por qué?*   how?

PRACTICE EXERCISE 6

Say whether the following statements are True or False.

1. T   F   Accent marks are optional.
2. T   F   An accent mark may change the stress of a word but not the meaning of it.
3. T   F   An accent mark may change the meaning of a word but not the stress.
4. T   F   An accent mark may change the meaning or the stress of a word.
5. T   F   Question words are seldom accentuated.
6. T   F   *Solo* means "alone
7. T   F   *Se* means "I know."
8. T   F   Accent marks sometimes indicate that there is an irregular stress pattern in a word.
9. T   F   *Sé* is a reflexive pronoun.
10. T   F   *Sólo* means "alone."

NOW, WATCH THE DVD

If you've digested the information in this part, you are ready to watch Section 4. And then, of course, come back to your book.

REVIEW EXERCISES
Now that you've gone through the section in the book, and then watched it on the DVD, here's a chance to show what you know.

REVIEW EXERCISE 1
Give the Spanish translation of each of the following words.

1. crazy
2. name
3. new
4. rose
5. way
6. coffee
7. lunatic
8. hat
9. American way
10. Colombian coffee
11. shoe
12. sugar
13. fingernail
14. war
15. cat
16. magic
17. orange

18. purse, bag
19. egg
20. thank you

REVIEW EXERCISE 2

Say whether the following statements are True or False.

1. T F The Spanish word for "I" is always capitalized.
2. T F An accent mark may change the meaning of the word, but not the stress.
3. T F When writing the date in Spanish you capitalize the month of the year.
4. T F An accent mark may change the meaning of the word.
5. T F A noun that refers to a person's nationality is not capitalized unless it is at the beginning of a sentence.
6. T F In Spanish, you always capitalize the first letter of the first word in a title of a book.
7. T F Colombian coffee is translated as *Colombiano café*.
8. T F Names of days of the week are not capitalized unless they are at the beginning of a sentence.
9. T F An accent mark may change the stress of the word.
10. T F The letter G in the words *gato, gracias, gordo* and *regalo* is pronounced like a hard G.
11. T F The letter H is pronounced like a J in English.
12. T F The letters B and V in the words *venir, bueno, vaca* and *burro* have the same sound.
13. T F *Tetera* means teapot.
14. T F The word *pelo* has a "y" sound in it.
15. T F The diphthong UI sounds like a quick oo + ee, or something like "wee".."

REVIEW EXERCISE 3

Practice aloud reading the following phrases out loud:

1. *el modo americano*
2. *café colombiano*
3. *el nombre de la rosa*
4. *La Mujer Maravilla*
5. *Estados Unidos de América*

REVIEW EXERCISE 4

Fill in the blanks for each of the Spanish words below.

1. Most people drink a cup of hot __ __ __ __ in the morning.
2. The man from Colombia is *el hombre* __ __ __ __ __ __ __ __ __ __ __.
3. You wear a __ __ __ __ __ __ __ __ __ __ on your head.
4. Lunatic ant is *la* __ __ __ __ __ __ __ __ __ *loca.*
5. The opposite of slow is __ __ __ __ __ __ __.
6. The name for the fruit and the color is __ __ __ __ __ __ __ __.
7. You need __ __ __ __ __ __ __ __ __ __ __ in order to make guacamole.
8. Train in Spanish is __ __ __ __ __ __ __ __ __ __ __ __ __.
9. He has no table manners, after dinner he let out a loud __ __ __ __ __ __ __.
10. These Antarctic birds like to dress up in tuxedos:

    — — — — — — — — — —.

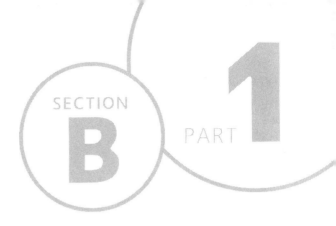

Answer Key

PRACTICE EXERCISE 1

1. loco – crazy or lunatic
2. rosa – rose
3. yo – I
4. nuevo – new
5. café – coffee
6. clavel – carnation
7. tulipán – tulip
8. costarricense – Costa Rican
9. dominicano – Dominican
10. peruano – Peruvian
11. cubano – Cuban
12. modo – way
13. mujer – woman
14. maravilla – wonder
15. té – tea

PRACTICE EXERCISE 2

1. A person from Costa Rica is a costarricense.
2. If you were born in the Dominican Republican, you are dominicano.
3. The guy who's acting crazy is very loco.
4. The American Way in Spanish is el modo americano.
5. Most people drink a cup of hot café in the morning.
6. The man from Colombia is el hombre colombiano.
7. Because of his nationality, Fidel Castro is cubano.
8. In England drinking té is more common than coffee.
9. When traveling in the Netherlands you are likely to encounter a tulipán.
10. The Spanish word for carnation is clavel.

PRACTICE EXERCISE 3

1. TRUE
2. TRUE
3. FALSE (maravilla)
4. FALSE (yo means "I.")
5. TRUE
6. TRUE
7. FALSE
8. FALSE
9. TRUE
10. FALSE

PRACTICE EXERCISE 4

1. "Harry Potter" es un libro de J. K. Rowling.
2. Yo soy una persona.
3. La persona soy yo.

4. El presidente Lincoln es un presidente importante.
5. Buenos Aires, Lima, Caracas y Santiago son ciudades de América Latina.
6. Luisa es una señora colombiana.
7. Hoy es lunes 13 de febrero.
8. "El nombre de la rosa" es un libro de Umberto Eco.
9. San Juan es la capital de Puerto Rico.
10. La Mujer Maravilla no es la presidenta de los Estados Unidos de América.

PRACTICE EXERCISE 5
1. ¿cuándo? – when?
2. ¿quién? – who?
3. ¿dónde? – where?
4. ¿qué? – what?
5. ¿cómo? – how?
6. ¿por qué? – why?

PRACTICE EXERCISE 6
1. FALSE
2. FALSE (It may change the meaning, too.)
3. FALSE (It may change the stress, too.)
4. TRUE
5. FALSE
6. TRUE
7. FALSE (Sé means "I know.")
8. TRUE
9. FALSE (Se is the pronoun.)
10. FALSE (Sólo means "only.")

REVIEW EXERCISE 1

1. crazy – loco
2. name – nombre
3. new – nuevo
4. rose – rosa
5. way – modo
6. coffee – café
7. lunatic – loco
8. hat – sombrero
9. American way – modo americano
10. Colombian Coffee – café colombiano
11. shoe – zapato
12. sugar – azúcar
13. fingernail – uña
14. war – guerra
15. cat – gato
16. magic – magia
17. orange – naranja
18. purse, bag – bolsa
19. egg – huevo
20. thank you – gracias

REVIEW EXERCISE 2

1. FALSE
2. FALSE (It may change both.)
3. FALSE
4. TRUE
5. TRUE
6. TRUE
7. FALSE (It's café colombiano.)

8. TRUE

9. TRUE

10. TRUE

11. FALSE (It's silent.)

12. TRUE

13. TRUE

14. FALSE

15. TRUE

REVIEW EXERCISE 4

1. Most people drink a cup of hot café in the morning.

2. The man from Colombia is el hombre colombiano.

3. You wear a sombrero on your head.

4. Lunatic ant is la hormiga loca.

5. The opposite of slow is rápido.

6. The name for the fruit and the color is naranja.

7. You need aguacates in order to make guacamole.

8. Train in Spanish is ferrocarril.

9. He has no table manners, after dinner he let out a loud eructo.

10. These Antarctic birds like to dress up in tuxedos: pingüinos.

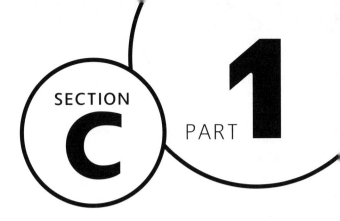

SECTION **C** PART **1**

Numbers 0-99

In this section we're going to learn how to count from 0 to 99. Don't worry, you won't have to view the tape 99 times in order to learn the numbers. It's really not that difficult. After you learn the numbers zero to thirty, you will notice a pattern that will be repeated into the forties, fifties, sixties and so on. But before we get into the specifics, let's learn some new vocabulary. And, now that you've learned such perfect pronunciation, there won't be any more of those crazy phonetics. But don't worry; if you're a bit unsure of how to pronounce something, it'll be on the DVD.

POINT 1: VOCABULARY

puntos – points

pato – duck

abogados – lawyers

dentistas – dentists

plantas – plants

tostador – toaster

tazas – cups

manzanas – apples

escritores – writers

árboles – trees

mesa – table

profesores – professors

doctores – doctors

examen – test

oveja – sheep

cero – zero

uno – one

dos – two

tres – three

cuatro – four

cinco – five

seis – six

siete – seven

ocho – eight

nueve – nine

diez – ten

once – eleven

doce – twelve

trece – thirteen

catorce – fourteen

quince – fifteen

dieciséis – sixteen

diecisiete – seventeen

dieciocho – eighteen

diecinueve – nineteen

veinte – twenty

veintiuno – twenty-one

veintidós – twenty-two

veintitrés – twenty-three

veinticuatro – twenty-four

veinticinco – twenty-five

treinta – thirty

cuarenta – forty

cincuenta – fifty

sesenta – sixty

setenta – seventy

ochenta – eighthy

noventa – ninety

PRACTICE EXERCISE 1

Match the Spanish word in the left column with the English word in the right column.

1. *puntos*   writers
2. *abogados*   six
3. *plantas*   four
4. *tazas*   sheep
5. *escritores*   points

6. *mesa*	seventy
7. *doctores*	test
8. *tres*	forty
9. *trece*	ninety
10. *ocho*	seven
11. *seis*	eight
12. *setenta*	doctors
13. *cuatro*	three
14. *cincuenta*	thirteen
15. *quince*	plants
16. *oveja*	fifteen
17. *examen*	table
18. *cuarenta*	fifty
19. *noventa*	lawyers
20. *siete*	cups

PRACTICE EXERCISE 2

Fill in the blanks for each of the Spanish words below.

1. Please bring me two *t __ __ __ s*, Roberto wants a cup of *c __ __ é* and Lucía wants a cup of *__ é*.
2. There were *setenta* screaming *__ b __ g __ d __ s* in the Court House.
3. There are *__ r __ s* Musketeers.
4. Shakespeare, Wilde and Woolf are *__ s __ r __ t __ r __ s*.
5. *Cincuenta* plus *diez* is *__ e __ e __ t __*.
6. Dinner is served, come sit at the *__ e __ __*.
7. What a slow gamel The basketball team ended up scoring *tres p __ n __ __ s*.

8. Friday 13th in Spanish is *viernes t __ __ __ e.*
9. In the Amazon you find thousands of species of flowers and *p __ a __ __ __ s.*
10. My tooth hurts, I need to visit my *__ e __ t __ __ __ a.*

POINT 2: NUMBERS 0-10

You probably already know the numbers 0 to 10 in Spanish. But in case you forgot them, here they are again.

0	*cero*
1	*uno*
2	*dos*
3	*tres*
4	*cuatro*
5	*cinco*
6	*seis*
7	*siete*
8	*ocho*
9	*nueve*
10	*diez*

PRACTICE EXERCISE 3

Try pronouncing all the numbers aloud. Practice the difficult sound of r in *tres* and *cuatro*. Also, watch out for the diphthongs in *cuatro, seis, siete* and *nueve*.

Uno Dos Tres Cuatro Cinco Seis Siete Ocho Nueve Diez

PRACTICE EXERCISE 4

Let's practice a little bit of arithmetic. Give the Spanish number for each arithmetic sentence.

1. Two multiplied by five is _____
2. Two minus two is _____
3. *Cuatro* plus *tres* is _____
4. *Dos* multiplied by *tres* is _____
5. *Ocho* minus *tres* is _____
6. *Siete* minus *seis* is _____
7. *Dos* multiplied by *dos* is _____
8. *Nueve* minus *seis* is _____
9. *Seis* plus *dos* is _____
10. *Diez* minus *dos* plus *uno* is _____
11. *Ocho* minus *siete* plus *uno* is _____
12. *Diez* divided by *dos* is _____
13. The sum of *tres* and *tres* is _____
14. *Nueve* minus *cinco* is _____
15. *Cero* multiplied by *cero* is _____

POINT 3: ONE = *UNO, UN, UNA*

"Now, wait a minute! Didn't you say that the Spanish word for one is *uno*?" Well yes and no. In the Spanish language "one" can be *uno*, *un* or *una*. There are, however, differences between *uno*, *un* and *una*; it all depends on how you're using the number.

When counting numbers you use the basic word for one, *uno*. Let's say you are counting one to ten because you are bored and have nothing else to do (or ten million if you have a lot of time to spare). In this case you say, *uno, dos, tres, cuatro* . . . until you get to ten (or ten million). Now, remember, you only use *uno* when you are counting numbers, you would not use it to count sheep at night or to count the tests that you failed last semester.

Let's move on to the second case. The word *un* also means one. Let's say that even though you didn't study at all last semester for your art history class, you managed to fail only one test. In that case, you would say *Suspendí sólo un examen* (I failed only one test). In this case you use the word *un* because it is followed by a masculine noun. You say *un examen*, not *uno examen*. (Remember, you use *uno* only when counting numbers, not people, places or things.) And what's this about a masculine noun? Well, we'll get into the rules of gender later, but for now you only need to know that, generally, if the word ends in "o" or in a consonant, it is a masculine word; if it ends in "a," it's a feminine word. This isn't always the same thing as gender in the sense of male or female – it's more of a grammatical category.

Now let's move to the third case, when "one" is *una*. Let's say that you failed many tests and you can't sleep at night. So you decide to count sheep. As the first sheep jumps the fence you say *una oveja*. In this case, "one sheep" uses the word *una*, the third way of saying "one" in Spanish. We use the word *una* because unlike the word *examen*, *oveja* is a feminine word. Remember the general rule of gender: If it ends in "a," it's likely to be a feminine word.

Not difficult, right? Let's recap. The number "one" has three different forms in Spanish: *uno, un* and *una. Uno* is used whenever you're simply counting. You use this form if there is no noun after it. The word *un* is used before a masculine noun such as *examen*. The word *una* is used before a feminine noun such as *oveja*. It's that simple!

And remember, this only happens with the number one. All the other numbers have only one form, whether you are simply counting numbers or whether you are counting masculine or feminine nouns. If you want to say that you flunked ten tests you say *Suspendí diez exámenes* and when the tenth sheep jumps the fence, you say *Diez ovejas*.

PRACTICE EXERCISE 5
Write the correct number before each noun. If there is no noun after the number, simply write the number in Spanish.

1.	five writers	_ _ _ _ _ _ *escritores*
2.	nine sheep	_ _ _ _ _ _ *ovejas*
3.	eight professors	_ _ _ _ _ p r _ _ e _ o _ _ s
4.	one doctor	_ _ _ _ c _ o _
5.	seven trees	_ _ _ _ _ _ _ r _ _ l _ _
6.	one table	_ _ _ _ _ _ s _
7.	two cups	_ _ _ _ _ _ z _ _
8.	six lawyers	_ _ _ _ _ _ _ _ _ g _ _ o _
9.	one plant	_ _ _ _ _ _ _ _ _ _
10.	four apples	_ _ _ _ _ _ _ _ _ _ _ _ _ _ _
11.	one toaster	_ _ _ _ _ _ _ _ _ _ _
12.	one duck	_ _ _ _ _ _ _
13.	seven	_ _ _ _ _ _
14.	one	_ _ _
15.	six	_ _ _ _

PRACTICE EXERCISE 6

Let's practice some more arithmetic. Say in Spanish how many people or objects there are.

1. Two lawyers joined four lawyers. There are _____ abogados.
2. We both had one table, and the waiter allowed us to join them. There are _____ mesas.
3. I bought six apples and ate two. There are _____ manzanas.
4. Five sheep were joined by four sheep. There are _____ o __ __ __ __ __ .
5. *I had one toaster but now I have none. There is _____ _____.*
6. One duck joined nine ducks. There are _____ _____.
7. There were two writers in the room but one just left. There is _____
8. I had eight plants but one died. There are _____ _____.
9. Two dentists joined one dentist. There are _____ _____.
10. There were *seis* cups before the boy broke *cinco*. There is _____ _____.

By now you're probably comfortable with the numbers *uno* to *diez*. Let's move on to the next group, numbers 11 to 20. These numbers follow an irregular pattern, just like what happens in English. You've probably noticed that in English, the number eleven doesn't look like twenty-one, thirty-one or forty-one. Well, the same happens in Spanish. Let's look at the first group, numbers 11 to 15:

11	*once*
12	*doce*
13	*trece*
14	*catorce*
15	*quince*

You may have noticed a resemblance to their single digit counterparts, for example, *doce* has a similar sound as *dos* (two) and *trece* sounds like *tres* (three).

Now let's look at the numbers 16 to 19:

16	*dieciséis*
17	*diecisiete*
18	*dieciocho*
19	*diecinueve*

You may have noticed a pattern in these numbers. You probably realized that they all begin with *dieci* followed by a single digit. The origin of *dieci* is *diez y*, which literally means "ten and." So in Spanish, *dieciocho* literally means "ten and eight."

Finally, there is twenty, our last number in this section:

20   *veinte*

PRACTICE EXERCISE 7

Say the Spanish equivalent of each:

1. twenty hats   _ _ _ _ _ _ _ _ _ _ _ _ _ _ _ s
2. twelve roses   _ _ _ _ _ _ _ _ _ a s
3. fourteen coffees   _ _ _ _ _ _ _ _ _ _ _ _ s
4. nineteen tests   _ _ _ _ _ _ _ _ _ _ _
                         _ _ _ _ _ _ _ e s
5. thirteen professors _ _ _ _ _ _ _ _ _ _ _ _ _ _ e s
6. three professors   _ _ _ _ _ _ _ _ _ _ _ _ _ _
7. fifteen doctors   _ _ _ _ _ _ _ _ _ _ _ _ _ e s
8. eleven lunatics   _ _ _ _ _ _ _ _ _ _ s
9. seventeen points   _ _ _ _ _ _ _ _ _ _ _ _ _ _ _ _ s
10. sixteen sheep   _ _ _ _ _ _ _ _ _ _ _ _ _ _ _ s

POINT 5: NUMBERS 20-99

You can relax now! The rest of the numbers are very easy to remember. You only need to learn the multiples of ten (twenty, thirty, forty . . .). The rest is very simple. First let's look at the numbers counting by ten:

20   *veinte*
30   *treinta*
40   *cuarenta*

50	*cincuenta*
60	*sesenta*
70	*setenta*
80	*ochenta*
90	*noventa*

For numbers 21 to 29, you need to do what we did with numbers 16 to 19. Remember how those numbers began with *dieci*? Well, numbers 21 to 29 begin with *veinti*. Notice that it is *veinti*, not "venti" which is the name of a type of coffee, or wait . . . it's the Italian word for twenty. So, to make numbers 21 to 29, you just need to tack on a single digit after *veinti*. So, for example, number twenty-four is formed by adding *cuatro* to *veinti*: *veinticuatro*. It is that simple . . . piece of cake!

Here you have numbers twenty to twenty-nine:

20	*veinte*
21	*veintiuno*
22	*veintidós*
23	*veintitrés*
24	*veinticuatro*
25	*veinticinco*
26	*veintiséis*
27	*veintisiete*
28	*veintiocho*
29	*veintinueve*

From thirty on, the numbers are even easier. You need to write three words: first the word for the appropriate multiple of ten, followed by the word *y* ("and"), followed by the single digit number. So, number 33 is *treinta y tres*, 45 is *cuarenta y cinco*, 56 is *cincuenta y seis*, and of course, 68 is *sesenta y ocho*. Ready for some practice?

PRACTICE EXERCISE 8
Give the Spanish number for each:

1. 77
2. 54
3. 23
4. 85
5. 42
6. 67
7. 89
8. 12
9. 2
10. 21
11. 41
12. 57
13. 79
14. 25
15. 32
16. 48
17. 0
18. 15

NOW, WATCH THE DVD

If you've digested the information in this part, you're ready to watch Section 5. Enjoy!

REVIEW EXERCISES
Now that you've gone through the section in the book, and then watched it on the DVD, here's a chance to show what you know.

REVIEW EXERCISE 1
Give the Spanish equivalent for each word.

1. writers
2. table
3. trees
4. dentists
5. plants
6. name
7. cups
8. doctors
9. points
10. lawyers
11. duck
12. professors
13. apples
14 test
15. new
16. eye

17. cow
18. city
19. glove
20. key

REVIEW EXERCISE 2

Ready to do some math? Give the Spanish word for each arithmetic problem.

1. The sum of *diez* and *veinte* is _____.
2. *Cuarenta* plus *cuatro* is _____.
3. *Veinticinco* minus *seis* is _____.
4. *Ocho* times *diez* is _____.
5. *Treinta* divided by *seis* is _____.
6. *Noventa* y *dos* plus *siete* is _____.
7. *Dos* plus *diez* is _____.
8. *Veinte* plus *veinticuatro* is _____.
9. *Cincuenta* minus *once* is _____.
10. *Cuatro* plus *tres* is _____.
11. *Catorce* plus *trece* is _____.
12. *Siete* plus *seis* minus *uno* is _____.
13. *Cuarenta* minus *siete* is _____.
14. *Cinco* times *cinco* is _____.
15. *Diecinueve* minus *ocho* is _____.
16. *Sesenta* plus *diecisiete* is _____.
17. *Ochenta* y *seis* minus *veintiséis* is _____.
18. *Cuarenta* minus *veinticinco* is _____.
19. *Dos* plus *dos* minus *cuatro* is _____.
20. *Tres* times *ocho* is _____.

REVIEW EXERCISE 3

Give the Spanish equivalent of the numbers below:

1. 1
2. 11
3. 21
4. 31
5. 41
6. 51
7. 61
8. 71
9. 81
10. 91

REVIEW EXERCISE 4

Say whether the following statements are True or False.

1. T F *Setenta* plus *diez* is *sesenta*.
2. T F *Escritores* means writers.
3. T F *Trece* is number three.
4. T F *Doce* is number twelve.
5. T F Both the fruit and the color are called *naranja*.
6. T F The letters B and V are pronounced differently.
7. T F Generally, we do not capitalize the adjective for nationalities.
8. T F Question words don't have accent marks.
9. T F An accent mark may change the stress and meaning of a word.
10. T F One plant is *un planta*.

11. T   F   Number eleven is *diez y uno*.

12. T   F   *Treinta* plus *diez* is *cuatro*.

13. T   F   Sixty-nine is *sesenta noventa*.

14. T   F   *Cincuenta* minus *doce* is *treinta y ocho*.

15. T   F   When counting numbers you begin by saying *un*.

Answer Key

PRACTICE EXERCISE 1

1. puntos – puntos
2. abogados – lawyers
3. plantas – plants
4. tazas – cups
5. escritores – writers
6. mesa – table
7. doctores – doctors
8. tres – three
9. trece – thirteen
10. ocho – eight
11. seis – six
12. setenta – seventy
13. cuatro – four
14. cincuenta – fifty

15. quince – fifteen
16. oveja – sheep
17. examen – test
18. cuarenta – forty
19. noventa – ninety
20. siete – seven

PRACTICE EXERCISE 2

1. Please bring me two tazas, Roberto wants a cup of café and Lucía wants a cup of té.
2. There were setenta screaming abogados in the Court House.
3. There are tres Musketeers.
4. Shakespeare, Wilde and Woolf are escritores.
5. Cincuenta plus diez is sesenta.
6. Dinner is served, come sit at the mesa.
7. What a slow game! The basketball team ended up scoring tres puntos.
8. Friday 13th in Spanish is viernes trece.
9. In the Amazon you find thousands of species of flowers and plantas.
10. My tooth hurts, I need to visit my dentista.

PRACTICE EXERCISE 4

1. Two multiplied by five is diez.
2. Two minus two is cero.
3. Cuatro plus tres is siete.
4. Dos multiplied by tres is seis.
5. Ocho minus tres is cinco.
6. Siete minus seis is uno.
7. Dos multiplied by dos is cuatro.
8. Nueve minus seis is tres.

9. Seis plus dos is ocho.
10. Diez minus dos plus uno is nueve.
11. Ocho minus siete plus uno is dos.
12. Diez divided by dos is cinco.
13. The sum of tres and tres is seis.
14. Nueve minus cinco is cuatro.
15. Cero multiplied by cero is cero.

PRACTICE EXERCISE 5

1. five writers – cinco escritores
2. nine sheep – nueve ovejas
3. eight professors – ocho profesores
4. one doctor – un doctor
5. seven trees – siete árboles
6. one table – una mesa
7. two cups – dos tazas
8. six lawyers – seis abogados
9. one plant – una planta
10. four apples – cuatro manzanas
11. one toaster – un tostador
12. one duck – un pato
13. seven – siete
14. one – uno
15. six – seis

PRACTICE EXERCISE 6

1. Two lawyers joined four lawyers. There are seis abogados.
2. We both had one table, and the waiter allowed us to join them. There are dos mesas.
3. I bought six apples and ate two. There are cuatro manzanas.

4. Five sheep were joined by four sheep. There are nueve ovejas.
5. I had one toaster but now I have none. There is cero tostador.
6. One duck joined nine ducks. There are diez patos.
7. There were two writers in the room but one just left. There is un escritor.
8. I had eight plants but one died. There are siete plantas.
9. Two dentists joined one dentist. There are tres dentistas.
10. There were seis cups before the boy broke cinco. There is una taza.

PRACTICE EXERCISE 7

1. twenty hats – veinte sombreros
2. twelve roses – doce rosas
3. fourteen coffees – catorce cafés
4. nineteen tests – diecinueve exámenes
5. thirteen professors – trece profesores
6. three professors – tres profesores
7. fifteen doctors – quince doctores
8. eleven lunatics – once locos
9. seventeen points – diecisiete puntos
10. sixteen sheep – dieciséis ovejas

PRACTICE EXERCISE 8

1. 77   setenta y siete
2. 54   cincuenta y cuatro
3. 23   veintitrés
4. 85   ochenta y cinco
5. 42   cuarenta y dos
6. 67   sesenta y siete
7. 89   ochenta y nueve
8. 12   doce

9.	2	dos
10.	21	veintiuno
11.	41	cuarenta y uno
12.	57	cincuenta y siete
13.	79	setenta y nueve
14.	25	veinticinco
15.	32	treinta y dos
16.	48	cuarenta y ocho
17.	0	cero
18.	15	quince

REVIEW EXERCISE 1

1. writers – escritores
2. table – mesa
3. trees – árboles
4. dentists – dentistas
5. plants – plantas
6. name – nombre
7. cups – tazas
8. doctors – doctores
9. points – puntos
10. lawyers – abogados
11. duck – pato
12. professors – profesores
13. apples – manzanas
14. test – examen
15. new – nuevo
16. eye – ojo
17. cow – vaca
18. city – ciudad

19. glove – guante
20. key – llave

REVIEW EXERCISE 2

1. The sum of diez and veinte is treinta.
2. Cuarenta plus cuatro is cuarenta y cuatro.
3. Veinticinco minus seis is diecinueve.
4. Ocho times diez is ochenta.
5. Treinta divided by seis is cinco.
6. Noventa y dos plus siete is noventa y nueve.
7. Dos plus diez is doce.
8. Veinte plus veinticuatro is cuarenta y cuatro.
9. Cincuenta minus once is treinta y nueve.
10. Cuatro plus tres is siete.
11. Catorce plus trece is veintisiete.
12. Siete plus seis minus uno is doce.
13. Cuarenta minus siete is treinta y tres.
14. Cinco times cinco is veinticinco.
15. Diecinueve minus ocho is once.
16. Sesenta plus diecisiete is setenta y siete.
17. Ochenta y seis minus veintiséis is sesenta.
18. Cuarenta minus veinticinco is quince.
19. Dos plus dos minus cuatro is cero.
20. Tres times ocho is veinticuatro.

REVIEW EXERCISE 3

1. 1   uno
2. 11   once
3. 21   veintiuno
4. 31   treinta y uno

5.	41	cuarenta y uno
6.	51	cincuenta y uno
7.	61	sesenta y uno
8.	71	setenta y uno
9.	81	ochenta y uno
10.	91	noventa y uno

REVIEW EXERCISE 4

1. FALSE
2. TRUE
3. FALSE
4. TRUE
5. TRUE
6. FALSE
7. TRUE
8. FALSE
9. TRUE
10. FALSE
11. FALSE
12. FALSE
13. FALSE
14. TRUE
15. FALSE

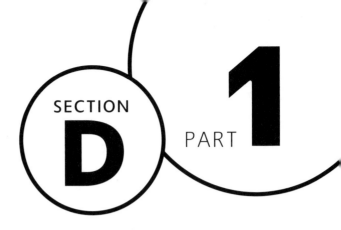

Honey, We Need to Talk (Greetings)

In this section we're going to learn different greetings, ways of saying goodbye, and various other pleasantries. These phrases are very important if you want to grab people's attention when you speak to them. Otherwise, they'll think that you are rude or simply *loco* and you'll run the risk of being ignored. These are very important phrases that are used in any language and will make you sound polite and genteel. Regardless of whether you are a very refined person or a sloppy brute, you'll need to use them if you want people to pay attention to you!

But first, let's take a look at the vocabulary that we'll use in this section.

clase – class

¿A dónde vas? – Where are you going?

Tengo que estudiar. – I have to study.

¿Para qué clase? – For what class?

historia – history

matemáticas – math

biología – biology

economía – economics

también – also

¡Tengo prisa! – I'm in a rush!

¡Nos vemos! – See you later!

Está bien. – Okay.

¿Qué haces hoy? – What are you doing today?

mañana – tomorrow

¡Qué sorpresa! – What a surprise!

Me llamo... – My name is . . .

¿Cómo te llamas? – What's your name?

Te presento a... – Let me introduce you to . . .

Mucho gusto. – It's nice to meet you.

Encantado. – I'm delighted to meet you.

Buenos días – Good morning

Buenas tardes – Good afternoon

Buenas noches – Good night

¡Hola! – Hi!

¿Cómo está? – How are you? (polite)

¿Cómo estás? – How are you? (friendly)

Bien gracias. ¿Y tú? – Fine, thank you. And you?

¿Qué tal? – How are you?

No muy bien. ¿Y tú? – Not very well. And you?

¿Cómo te va? – How is it going?

Muy bien. – Very well.

Regular. – Not so well.

Así, así. – So, so.

Muy mal. – Very badly.

Adiós – Goodbye

Hasta luego. – Until later.

Ciao – Goodbye

You may have already noticed that in Spanish there are several different ways to greet a person or say goodbye. The phrases that you'll use depend on the situation and the level of formality. You are likely to start any conversation by saying good morning, afternoon or evening. To say "good morning" you say *buenos días*, "good afternoon" is *buenas tardes* and "good evening" is *buenas noches*. You also say *buenas noches* if you want to say "good night," there's no distinction between the two in Spanish. To say "How are you?" to an adult or someone that you don't know very well, you would say ¿*Cómo está*? Of course, you can also simply say *Hola*, which means "Hi."

Here are some less formal greetings. You are most likely to use these with friends and family. The three expressions are very similar in meaning. To say "How are you?" you say ¿*Cómo estás*? There's another greeting that is even less formal and also means "How are you?" To greet someone very informally you would say ¿*Qué tal*?

You can also say *¿Cómo te va?* which is the most informal of the three and it means "How is it going?"

There are several ways to introduce oneself to others. To introduce yourself without the help of somebody else you need to go up to the person and use the phrase *Me llamo . . .* which means "My name is . . ." Depending on how happy the person is to see you, the person may decide to reciprocate warmly by saying *Me llamo . . .* back to you. Or, if you're too pushy or have bad breath or something, the person may decide to remain silent (or run away). If you're very persistent, you will need to ask *¿Cómo te llamas?*, which means "What is your name?" Then you may get a name. Or you may get no response other than *¡Adiós!* which of course means "Goodbye!" We'll come back to different ways of saying goodbye in a second . . . If you want to be a matchmaker and introduce someone to another person, you would need to say *Te presento a . . .* which means "Let me introduce you to . . ."

There are several different ways of saying goodbye in Spanish. Again, the phrase that you will use depends on the level of formality of the situation. The most common way is a simple *Adiós*, which means "Goodbye." Another common expression is *Hasta luego,* which literally means "Until later." A more informal variation of *Hasta luego* is *Nos vemos,* which means "See you later." The most informal variation is *Ciao. Ciao* is the Italian word for goodbye, but it is also widely used in Spanish.

Now that you've looked at different greetings, introductions and ways of saying goodbye, take a look at these practice exercises.

PRACTICE EXERCISE 1

Match the Spanish word in the left column with the English word in the right column. To make it more challenging, all exclamation or question marks have been eliminated.

1. *adiós*   class
2. *buenas noches*   I'm in a rush!
3. *mañana*   good afternoon
4. *me llamo*   so, so
5. *también*   fine, thanks
6. *cómo estás*   goodbye
7. *clase*   good evening/good night
8. *así, así*   how are you? (friendly)
9. *bien, gracias*   how are you? (polite)
10. *hola*   also
11. *está bien*   let me introduce you to
12. *buenos días*   I'm delighted to meet you
13. *tengo prisa*   hi
14. *cómo está*   okay
15. *te presento a*   how is it going?
16. *encantado*   my name is
17. *buenas tardes*   tomorrow
18. *cómo te va*   good morning

PRACTICE EXERCISE 2

Fill in the blanks in the following dialogue with the appropriate Spanish word or phrases.

María and Susana are walking to class when they run into Carlos. María introduces Carlos to Susana. Then María leaves when she realizes she's late for class. Carlos is very happy to meet Susana. Susana finds him annoying and pushy, and she walks away in the middle of the conversation.

María: _____ (Hello), *Carlos.*

¡_____ _____!
(What a surprise!)

¿_____ _____?
(How are you?-friendly form)

Carlos: _____ (Hello), *María.*

_____ (Fine), *gracias,*

¿_____ _____?
(and you?)

María: _____ _____ (Very well).

_____ _____

_____ (Let me introduce you to)

Susana.

But Carlos could not hear her very well.

Carlos: *Perdón,* ¿_____ _____

_____? (What's your name?)

Susana: _____ _____

_____ (My name is Susana).

Carlos is <u>very</u> happy to meet her.

Carlos: _____ (I'm delighted to meet you),
                 Susana.

Susana is not as happy to meet him but she decides to be polite.

Susana: _____ _____ (It's nice to
                 meet you), *Carlos.*

María decides to leave, she's late for her History class.

María: *Voy a la* _____ (class) *de*
                 _____ (History). ¡_____
                 _____! (I'm in a rush!)
Carlos: ¡_____ (Goodbye) *María!*
Susana: ¡_____ _____! (See you
                 later!)

Carlos is clearly interested in Susana. She's clearly not.

Carlos: ¿_____ _____
                 _____? (What are you doing today?)
Susana: _____ _____
                 _____ (I have to study.)
Carlos: ¿_____ _____
                 _____? (For what class?)
Susana: *Para la clase de* _____ (Economics)
Carlos: ¿Y _____? (tomorrow)

Susana:	_____ _____
	_____ (I have to study.)
Carlos:	¿_____ _____
	_____? (For what class?)
Susana:	*Para la clase de* _____ (Math)
Carlos:	*¿Necesitas estudiar para la clase de*
	_____? (Do you need to study for your
	Biology class?)
Susana:	_____ (goodbye).
	¡_____ _____! (I'm in
	a rush!)

> **POINT 2:** QUESTION MARKS, EXCLAMATION
> MARKS AND PERIODS

You probably noticed something unusual in the punctuation of the questions in the previous section. In case you weren't paying attention, here are some of the questions again: *¿Qué haces hoy? ¿A dónde vas? ¿Cómo te llamas? ¿Qué tal? ¿Y tú?*

You can see that there's an upside-down question mark at the beginning of each question. Well, that's not an error – it's the way that all questions begin in Spanish. This beginning question mark is actually quite useful when you're reading because it lets you know early on that you need to change the intonation of the sentence in order to turn it into a question. You should probably practice a few times how to write the upside down question mark, think of it as a lower case letter "c" with a dot on top of it: "¿". And don't forget, this upside-down question mark doesn't replace the regular question mark that also appears at the end of the question. You need to have both in order to write a question in Spanish.

Notice that the same happens with exclamation marks. Remember these expressions? *¡Hola! ¡Tengo prisa! ¡Nos vemos! ¡Qué sorpresa!* You use the same early warning system for exclamations as you do for questions. You need to have an upside-down exclamation mark at the beginning of a phrase or sentence that expresses surprise or emphasis. And once again, remember, this upside-down exclamation mark doesn't replace the right-side up exclamation mark at the end of the expression. To write the beginning exclamation mark, simply write the same line that you use for the exclamation mark but the period goes on top instead: (¡).

Here's the easy part about this section. There's nothing different about periods in Spanish. You place the periods at the end of a sentence to show that the sentence is finished. And don't forget what we learned about capitalization earlier in the book. In Spanish, as well as in English, you always begin a new sentence with a capital letter.

PRACTICE EXERCISE 3
This is the dialogue that we learned in this section. All exclamation marks, question marks and periods have been left out. Make all corrections that are necessary.

María:	*Hola, Carlos Qué sorpresa Cómo estás*
Carlos:	*Hola, María Bien gracias, y tú*
María:	*Muy bien, y tú Te presento a Susana*
Carlos:	*Perdón, cómo te llamas*

Susana:	*Me llamo Susana*
Carlos:	*Encantado, Susana*
Susana:	*Mucho gusto, Carlos*
María:	*Voy a la clase de historia Tengo prisa*
Carlos:	*Adiós, María*
Susana:	*Nos vemos*
Carlos:	*Qué haces hoy*
Susana:	*Tengo que estudiar*
Carlos:	*Para qué clase*
Susana:	*Para la clase de economía*
Carlos:	*Y mañana*
Susana:	*Tengo que estudiar*
Carlos:	*Para qué clase*
Susana:	*Para la clase de matemáticas*
Carlos:	*Necesitas estudiar para la clase de biología*
Susana:	*Adiós, tengo prisa*

PRACTICE EXERCISE 4

Correct the following dialogue by adding question marks, exclamation marks or periods. Make sure to write capital letters where they are needed.

carlos:	*hola a dónde vas, roberto*
roberto:	*voy a la clase de matemáticas, y tú*
carlos:	*tengo que estudiar*
roberto:	*para qué clase*
carlos:	*tengo que estudiar para la case de economía*
roberto:	*tengo prisa*
carlos:	*nos vemos*

NOW, WATCH THE DVD

If you've digested this information, turn on your DVD and watch Section 7.

REVIEW EXERCISES

Now that you've gone through the section in the book, and then watched it on the DVD, here's a chance to show what you know.

REVIEW EXERCISE 1

Give the Spanish translation of each of the following words or phrases.

1. class
2. I'm in a rush!
3. What are you doing today?
4. also
5. Good morning
6. So, so
7. Until later
8. Good afternoon
9. See you later
10. Goodbye
11. Good night
12. Hi
13. Not very well, and you?
14. How is it going?
15. Very well

REVIEW EXERCISE 2

Say whether the following statements are True or False.

1. T F   *Hasta luego* is a common expression that literally means "How are you?"
2. T F   *Nos vemos* is a way of saying goodbye that means "See you later."
3. T F   *Buenas tardes* means "Good night."
4. T F   You can say goodbye to someone by saying *Ciao*.
5. T F   *¿Cómo te va?* means "Are you in a rush?"
6. T F   At night you say *buenos días* but in the evening you say *buenas noches*.
7. T F   You can greet someone informally by saying *¿Qué tal?*
8. T F   At the end of a conversation you should say *Tengo prisa*.
9. T F   To introduce yourself to someone you would say *Me llamo . . .*
10. T F   After being introduced to a new person you should say *Adiós, perdedor.*

REVIEW EXERCISE 3

Give the Spanish translation of each of the following phrases.

1. Good afternoon, my name is Roberto.
2. Good evening, let me introduce you to Rosa.
3. Good morning Elena, where are you going?
4. See you later, class!
5. How is it going?
6. Hello! What is your name?
7. What a surprise!
8. How is it going? It's nice to meet you.

REVIEW EXERCISE 4

Fill in the blanks with the appropriate vocabulary words.

1. Fourteen coffees is _____ _____ s
2. Nineteen tests is _____ _____ e s
3. Thirteen professors is _____ _____ e s
4. Dos multiplied by tres is _____
5. Ocho minus tres is _____
6. Siete minus seis is ____.
7. Roberto wants a cup of c ___ é and Lucía wants a cup of __ é.
8. The word for coconuts is _____.
9. A _____ is a cat.
10. If something is fast, it's _____.

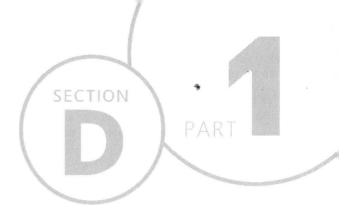

Answer Key

PRACTICE EXERCISE 1

1. adiós – goodbye
2. buenas noches – good evening/good night
3. mañana – tomorrow
4. me llamo – my name is
5. también – also
6. cómo estás – how are you? (friendly)
7. clase – class
8. así, así – so, so
9. bien, gracias – fine, thanks
10. hola – hi
11. está bien – okay
12. buenos días – good morning
13. tengo prisa – I'm in a rush!

14. cómo está – how are you? (polite)
15. te presento a – let me introduce you to
16. encantado – I'm delighted to meet you.
17. buenas tardes – good afternoon
18. cómo te va – how is it going?

PRACTICE EXERCISE 2

María:	Hola, (Hello) Carlos. ¡Qué sorpresa! (What a surprise!) ¿Cómo estás? (How are you? – friendly)
Carlos:	Hola (Hello), María. Bien (Fine), gracias, ¿ y tú? (and you?)
María:	Muy bien (Very well). Te presento a (Let me introduce you to) Susana.
Carlos:	Perdón, ¿cómo te llamas? (What's your name?)
Susana:	Me llamo Susana (My name is Susana).
Carlos:	Encantado (I'm delighted to meet you), Susana.
Susana:	Mucho gusto (It's nice to meet you), Carlos.
María:	Voy a la clase (class) de historia (History). ¡Tengo prisa!(I'm in a rush!)
Carlos:	¡Adiós, (Goodbye) María!
Susana:	¡Nos vemos! (See you later!)
Carlos:	¿Qué haces hoy? (What are you doing today?)
Susana:	Tengo que estudiar (I have to study).
Carlos:	¿Para qué clase? (For what class?)
Susana:	Para la clase de economía (Economics).
Carlos:	¿Y mañana? (tomorrow)
Susana:	Tengo que estudiar (I have to study).
Carlos:	¿Para qué clase? (For what class?)
Susana:	Para la clase de matemáticas (Math).

Carlos:	¿Necesitas estudiar para la clase de biología? (Do you need to study for your Biology class?)
Susana:	Adiós (goodbye), ¡tengo prisa! (I'm in a rush!)

PRACTICE EXERCISE 3

María:	Hola, Carlos. ¡Qué sorpresa! ¿Cómo estás?
Carlos:	Hola, María. Bien gracias, ¿y tú?
María:	Muy bien, ¿y tú? Te presento a Susana.
Carlos:	Perdón, ¿cómo te llamas?
Susana:	Me llamo Susana.
Carlos:	Encantado, Susana.
Susana:	Mucho gusto, Carlos.
María:	Voy a la clase de historia. ¡Tengo prisa!
Carlos:	¡Adiós, María!
Susana:	¡Nos vemos!
Carlos:	¿Qué haces hoy?
Susana:	Tengo que estudiar.
Carlos:	¿Para qué clase?
Susana:	Para la clase de economía.
Carlos:	¿Y mañana?
Susana:	Tengo que estudiar.
Carlos:	¿Para qué clase?
Susana:	Para la clase de matemáticas.
Carlos:	¿Necesitas estudiar para la clase de biología?
Susana:	Adiós, ¡tengo prisa!

PRACTICE EXERCISE 4

Carlos:	¡Hola! ¿A dónde vas, Roberto?
Roberto:	Voy a la clase de matemáticas, ¿y tú?
Carlos:	Tengo que estudiar.

Roberto:	¿Para qué clase?
Carlos:	Tengo que estudiar para la case de economía.
Roberto:	¡Tengo prisa!
Carlos:	¡Nos vemos!

REVIEW EXERCISE 1

1. class – clase
2. I'm in a rush! – ¡Tengo prisa!
3. What are you doing today? – ¿Qué haces hoy?
4. also – también
5. Good morning – Buenos días
6. So, so – Así, así
7. Until later – Hasta luego
8. Good afternoon – Buenas tardes
9. See you later – Nos vemos
10. Goodbye – Adiós
11. Good night – Buenas noches
12. Hi – Hola
13. Not very well, and you? – No muy bien, ¿y tú?
15. How is it going? – ¿Cómo te va?
16. Very well – Muy bien

REVIEW EXERCISE 2

1. FALSE
2. TRUE
3. FALSE
4. TRUE
5. FALSE
6. FALSE
7. TRUE

8. FALSE
9. TRUE
10. FALSE

REVIEW EXERCISE 3.

1. Buenas tardes, me llamo Roberto.
2. Buenas noches, te presento a Rosa.
3. Buenos días Elena, ¿a dónde vas?
4. ¡Nos vemos, clase!
5. ¿Cómo te va?
6. ¡Hola! ¿Cómo te llamas?
7. ¡Qué sorpresa!
8. ¿Cómo te va? Mucho gusto.

REVIEW EXERCISE 4

1. Fourteen coffees is catorce cafés.
2. Nineteen tests is diecinueve exámenes.
3. Thirteen professors is trece profesores.
4. Dos multiplied by tres is seis.
5. Ocho minus tres is cinco.
6. Siete minus seis is uno.
7. Roberto wants a cup of café and Lucía wants a cup of té.
8. The word for coconuts is cocos.
9. A gato is a cat.
10. If something is fast, it's rápido.

Articles and Pronouns

PART **2**

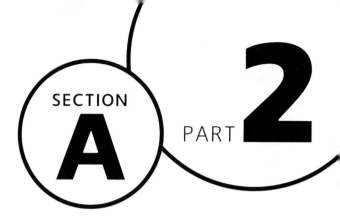

SECTION **A**

PART **2**

Articles

In this section we're going to learn how to use definite and indefinite articles. An article is a little word that precedes a noun and tells us a little bit about the word that it modifies. In English, the articles are "the," "a," "an" and "some." We'll discuss the use of articles in the next section but first let's look at some new vocabulary.

el – the (masculine-singular)

la – the (feminine-singular)

los – the (masculine-plural)

las – the (feminine-plural)

un – a or an (masculine-singular)

una – a or an (feminine-singular)

unos – some (masculine-plural)

unas – some (feminine-plural)

oreja – ear

camisa – shirt

guante – glove

mano – hand

hombro – shoulder

piano – piano

boca – mouth

problema – problem

mancha – spot

plato – plate

guitarrista – guitar player

pianista – pianist

clarinetista – clarinet player

violinista – violinist

flautista – flute player

PRACTICE EXERCISE 1

Match each of the Spanish words in the left column with the English meaning in the right column.

1. *la*   the (masculine-singular)
2. *camisa*   hand
3. *boca*   some (feminine-plural)
4. *unos*   shirt
5. *mancha*   a or an (masculine-singular)
6. *una*   ear
7. *el*   piano
8. *problema*   the (feminine-singular)
9. *mano*   spot
10. *los*   a or an (feminine-singular)
11. *hombro*   the (feminine-plural)
12. *un*   mouth
13. *piano*   shoulder
14. *guante*   the (masculine-plural)
15. *las*   problem
16. *unas*   glove
17. *oreja*   some (masculine-plural)

POINT 2: GENDER

In this section we're going to talk about gender. In Spanish, every noun is given a masculine or feminine gender. This is easy to understand as long as we're talking about people or animals. For example, *el señor* is masculine while *la señora* is feminine. If you hear that *el gato está loco* you know that the male cat is crazy, but if you hear *la gata está loca* you know that they're referring to a female cat. Notice that the word *loco* changes into *loca* when we describe the female cat, but you'll see more about that later.

So it's easy to understand gender in humans and animals, but what about inanimate objects? In Spanish, unlike in English, everything is either masculine or feminine. But don't think of this as male and female when it comes to inanimate objects – then it's more just like a grammatical category, or type. For example, your eye (*ojo*) is masculine (even if it's a woman's eye) but your ear (*oreja*) is feminine (even if it's a man's ear). Confused? The hat (*sombrero*) you're wearing is masculine but your shirt (*camisa*) is feminine. The glove (*guante*) you're wearing on your hand is masculine, but your hand (*mano*) is clearly feminine. Shoulder pain, anyone? Your shoulder (*hombro*) is masculine. Still confused? Oh, the guitar you're playing? The guitar (*guitarra*) is feminine, but a piano (*piano*) is masculine . . . Parking the car in your garage? Both of them (*coche* and *garaje*) are masculine. A rose, well a rose (*rosa*) is feminine. Is this making any sense? No? Not yet of course, but get ready to have it all sorted out!

There's nothing about each object that tells you whether it's masculine or feminine. Look at your ear, do you see anything that says it's a feminine object? Is there anything about a piano that indicates that it's masculine? What is it about an eye that would make it masculine? You can analyze as much as you'd like and you would not be able to come up with a very convincing answer. The answer to gender of inanimate objects lies on the ending of the word. In Spanish if a word ends in -o it generally is a masculine word. If the word ends in -a it generally is a feminine word. So the words *ojo, hombro, piano* and *sombrero* are masculine words because they end in -o. The words *oreja, camisa, guitarra*, and *rosa* are feminine words because they end in -a.

But notice that important word – "generally." That is because there are some exceptions to this rule. For example, the word hand or *mano* ends in -o but it is a feminine word. The word *problema* (problem) ends in "-a," yet it is a masculine word. And did you notice the word above that doesn't end in an –a or –o? It was glove, *guante*, and it's one of those –e ending words that can be either feminine or masculine. These exceptions are always a big *problema* for people learning a new languagel But for now, you should feel comfortable using this rule of thumb: if the word ends in -o it's masculine, if it ends in -a it's feminine.

PRACTICE EXERCISE 2

Give the Spanish word for each of the nouns below. After that, specify if it's a masculine or feminine noun.

1. egg
2. way
3. course
4. burp
5. car
6. gift
7. war
8. fingernail

9. apple

10. orange

11. shoe

12. cheese

13. point

14. cup

15. plant

16. dinner

17. hair

18. eye

19. plate

20. teapot

POINT 2: DEFINITE ARTICLES

Let's review a little bit of elementary grammar. Remember the different kinds of articles that you learned in your grammar class? No, not magazine or newspapers articles . . . We're talking about definite and indefinite articles such as "the," "a," "an" or "some." Articles are the little words that tell us a bit about the noun that follows.

Let's talk about definite articles first. A definite article specifies which thing, person, place or idea you're talking about. Let's say you're in the kitchen and want to clean up the mess you made after cooking a meal. But you don't want to clean up just any plate, you want to clean one plate in specific. Remember the word for plate? In case you forgot, it is *plato*. In this particular case you would refer to the plate as *el plato*. You're not talking about any old plate in the kitchen but one in particular. You're making it a "defined" plate – just like the name of the article suggests. You're being definite and specific. In English, there's only one definite article, the word "the." In Spanish there are four: *el, la, los* and *las*. You need to determine the gender and number of the noun, before deciding which one you're going to use. In the case of *plato* you may have already noticed that it is a masculine singular word. The masculine singular definite article is *el*.

Now, let's say that you want to clean a particular sticky spot in the kitchen. Remember the word for spot? In case you forgot, it is *mancha*. You probably noticed that it is a feminine word because it ends in the letter "-a." In Spanish, the feminine singular definite article is *la*, so you would refer to that specific sticky spot as *la mancha*. For those of you interested in geography or literature, *La Mancha* is the name of a region in central Spain that serves as the setting of the novel *Don Quixote* (spelled "Don Quijote" in Spanish) by Miguel de Cervantes.

Let's look at the plural cases now. If you want to clean a group of specific plates you would need to use the definite article *el* because plate is a masculine word, right? Not so! You see, in Spanish you need to look at both the *gender* and the *number* of the noun. So, if you want to clean a group of specific plates you would need to use a different definite article. The definite article that you use for a masculine plural noun is *los*. In this case "the plates" is *los platos*. Something similar happens with the feminine plural definite article. If you make a mess while cooking and notice many sticky spots you would say *las manchas*. The feminine plural definite article is *las*. Sounds confusing? Let's summarize then. In English there is only one definite article, "the." In Spanish, there are four: *el, la, los* and *las*. You need to determine both the gender and the number of the noun before deciding which one you need to use.

PRACTICE EXERCISE 3
Put the appropriate definite article (*el, la, los, las*) in front of each noun.

1. _____ *uñas*
2. _____ *vaca*
3. _____ *manzana*
4. _____ *eructo*
5. _____ *truchas*
6. _____ *cursos*
7. _____ *queso*
8. _____ *bolsa*
9. _____ *zapatos*
10. _____ *tetera*
11. _____ *curso*
12. _____ *ojo*
13. _____ *cena*
14. _____ *quesos*
15. _____ *tazas*
16. _____ *planta*
17. _____ *naranjas*
18. _____ *huevo*
19. _____ *pelo*
20. _____ *modos*

PRACTICE EXERCISE 4

Write the following nouns with their appropriate definite articles.

1. the cheeses _____ _____
2. the year _____ _____
3. the shoes _____ _____
4. the cars _____ _____
5. the course _____ _____
6. the gifts _____ _____
7. the dinner _____ _____
8. the apples _____ _____
9. the plants _____ _____
10. the bag _____ _____
11. the oranges _____ _____
12. the fingernails _____ _____
13. the war _____ _____
14. the guitar _____ _____
15. the hat _____ _____
16. the ducks _____ _____
17. the point _____ _____
18. the cows _____ _____
19. the teapot _____ _____
20. the eye _____ _____

POINT 3: INDEFINITE ARTICLES

There are three indefinite articles in English. Two of the articles are singular, "a" and "an," and one of them is plural, "some." In Spanish there are four indefinite article, *un, una, unos* and *unas*. Remember that articles are considered adjectives because they tell us a little bit about the noun that follows. In this case, they tell us whether the noun that follows is masculine or feminine or whether it is singular or plural.

What's the difference between definite and indefinite articles? Let's go back to that mess you made in the kitchen. Pretend that you have to clean up again but this time you're not being specific and you have time to clean only one plate. You can clean any plate, "a plate." Since you're not being specific, you need to use an indefinite article. You're not cleaning "the plate" you had in mind, you're cleaning "a plate." In this case you would say *un plato*. Since *plato* is a masculine singular word, you need to use the masculine singular indefinite article, *un*. Remember those sticky spots? Let's say again you have time to clean just one. Since *mancha* is a feminine singular word, you need to use the feminine singular indefinite article, *una*. In this case you would say *una mancha* or "a spot."

Now let's look at the plural cases. Let's say you want to wash some plates. You need to use the masculine plural indefinite article, *unos*. So, the plural of *un plato* or "a plate" becomes *unos platos* or "some plates." As for the sticky spots, you need to use the feminine plural indefinite article, *unas*. So, the plural of *una mancha* becomes *unas manchas* or "some spots."

PRACTICE EXERCISE 5
Put the appropriate indefinite article (*un, una, unos, unas*) in front of each noun.

1. _____ *cena*
2. _____ *ojos*

3. _____ *trucha*
4. _____ *patos*
5. _____*punto*
6. _____*manzanas*
7. _____ *taza*
8. _____ *cigüeña*
9. _____ *huevos*
10. _____ *naranja*
11. _____ *año*
12. _____ *vaca*
13. _____ *quesos*
14. _____ *zapatos*
15. _____ *teteras*
16. _____ *rosa*
17. _____ *sombreros*
18. _____ *bolsa*
19. _____ *uñas*
20. _____ *tazas*

PRACTICE EXERCISE 6

Write the following nouns with their appropriate indefinite articles.

1. some shoes _____ _____
2. an eye _____ _____
3. some cars _____ _____
4. some gifts _____ _____
5. a war _____ _____
6. a guitar _____ _____

7. some courses   _____ _____
8. a cow   _____ _____
9. some trouts   _____ _____
10. a hair   _____ _____
11. some burps   _____ _____
12. a dinner   _____ _____
13. an orange   _____ _____
14. some bags   _____ _____
15. a year   _____ _____
16. a fingernail   _____ _____
17. a teapot   _____ _____
18. some ways   _____ _____
19. a rose   _____ _____
20. some ducks   _____ _____

POINT 4: SUMMARY

Let's summarize definite and indefinite articles. Articles are like adjectives because they tell us a little bit of information about the noun, such as gender and number. In English there is only one definite article, "the." In Spanish, there are four definite articles: *el, la, los* and *las*. In English there are three indefinite articles: "a," "an" and "some." In Spanish, there are four: *un, una, unos* and *unas*. You need to determine the gender and number of the noun before deciding which definite or indefinite article to use.

DEFINITE ARTICLES

Masculine singular	el	el regalo	the gift
Feminine singular	la	la boca	the mouth
Masculine plural	los	los ojos	the eyes
Feminine plural	las	las camisas	the shirts

INDEFINITE ARTICLES

Masculine singular	un	un hombro	a shoulder
Feminine singular	una	una manzana	an apple
Masculine plural	unos	unos abogados	some lawyers
Feminine plural	unas	unas plantas	some plants

PRACTICE EXERCISE 7

Rewrite each noun with the opposite article. If there is an indefinite article, write it with a definite article. If there is a definite article, write it with an indefinite article.

Example: *una vaca*   *la vaca*

1. *unos cursos* _____ _____
2. *la tetera* _____ _____
3. *unos modos* _____ _____
4. *las rosas* _____ _____
5. *unos zapatos* _____ _____
6. *un huevo* _____ _____
7. *las bolsas* _____ _____
8. *una planta* _____ _____
9. *unos pingüinos* _____ _____
10. *la trucha* _____ _____
11. *unos carros* _____ _____
12. *los regalos* _____ _____
13. *una guerra* _____ _____
14. *los sombreros* _____ _____
15. *un ojo* _____ _____

(NOW, WATCH THE DVD)

If you've digested this information, turn on your DVD and watch Section 8.

REVIEW EXERCISES

Now that you've gone through the section in the book, and then watched it on the DVD, here's a chance to practice what you've learned.

REVIEW EXERCISE 1

Say who's who in the orchestra by writing the appropriate definite article in the blanks. Use the names for clues about gender and number.

1. _____ pianista es Ramón.
2. _____ violinistas son Felipe y Luis.
3. _____ guitarristas son Claudia y Carlos.
4. _____ clarinetista es Teresa.
5. _____ flautistas son Marta y Lucía.
6. _____ pianistas son Carolina y Ester.
7. _____ violinista es Jorge.
8. _____ guitarrista es Carmen.
9. _____ clarinetistas son Elena y Clara.
10. _____ flautista es Albita.

REVIEW EXERCISE 2

Now say their role in the orchestra by writing the appropriate indefinite article in the blank.

1. Ramón es _____ pianista.
2. Felipe y Luis son _____ violinistas.
3. Claudia y Carlos son _____ guitarristas.
4. Teresa es _____ clarinetista.
5. Paco y Roberto son _____ flautistas .

6. *Carolina y Juan son* _____ *pianistas.*
7. *Jorge es* _____ *violinista.*
8. *Carmen es* _____ *guitarrista.*
9. *Elena y Clara son* _____ *clarinetistas.*
10. *Albita es* _____ *flautista.*

REVIEW EXERCISE 3
Give the Spanish translations for each of the following words.

1. the (feminine-singular)
2. the (masculine-plural)
3. the (feminine-plural)
4. a or an (masculine-singular)
5. some (feminine-plural)
6. shirt
7. hand
8. shoulder
9. mouth
10. spot
11. plate
12. pianist

REVIEW EXERCISE 4
The people below are international students studying in the USA.
Express their nationality by writing the appropriate indefinite articles.

1. *(España) Manuel y Rafael son* _____ *estudiantes españoles.*
2. *(Puerto Rico) Silvia es* _____ *estudiante puertorriqueña.*

3. *(Cuba) Isabel y Beatriz son* _____ *estudiantes cubanas.*
4. *(México) Carlos es* _____ *estudiante mexicano.*
5. *(Honduras) Eduardo y Federico son* _____ *estudiantes hondureños.*
6. *(Argentina) Alberto y Lisa son* _____ *estudiantes argentinos.*
7. *(Chile) Gabriela es* _____ *estudiante chilena.*
8. *(Venezuela) Brenda y Luisa son* _____ *estudiantes venezolanas.*
9. *(Panamá) Roberto y Beatriz son* _____ *estudiantes panameños.*
10. *(Costa Rica) Ricardo es* _____ *estudiante costarricense.*

Answer Key

PRACTICE EXERCISE 1

1. la – the (feminine-singular)
2. camisa – shirt
3. boca – mouth
4. unos – some (masculine-plural)
5. mancha – spot
6. una – a or an (feminine-singular)
7. el – the (masculine-singular)
8. problema – problem
9. mano – hand
10. los – the (masculine-plural)
11. hombro – shoulder
12. un – a or an (masculine-singular)
13. piano – piano
14. guante – glove
15. las – the (feminine-plural)

16. unas – some (feminine-plural)
17. oreja – ear

PRACTICE EXERCISE 2

1. egg – huevo – M
2. way – modo – M
3. course – curso – M
4. burp – eructo – M
5. car – carro or coche – M
6. gift – regalo – M
7. war – guerra – F
8. fingernail – uña – F
9. apple – manzana – F
10. orange – naranja – F
11. shoe – zapato – M
12. cheese – queso – M
13. point – punto – M
14. cup – taza – F
15. plant – planta – F
16. dinner – cena – F
17. hair – pelo – M
18. eye – ojo – M
19. plate – plato – M
20. teapot – tetera – F

PRACTICE EXERCISE 3

1. las uñas
2. la vaca
3. la manzana
4. el eructo

5. las truchas

6. los cursos

7. el queso

8. la bolsa

9. los zapatos

10. la tetera

11. el curso

12. el ojo

13. la cena

14. los quesos

15. las tazas

16. la planta

17. las naranjas

18. el huevo

19. el pelo

20. los modos

PRACTICE EXERCISE 4

1. the cheeses – los quesos

2. the year – el año

3. the shoes – los zapatos

4. the cars – los carros or los coches

5. the course – el curso

6. the gifts – los regalos

7. the dinner – la cena

8. the apples – las manzanas

9. the plants – las plantas

10. the bag – la bolsa

11. the oranges – las naranjas

12. the fingernails – las uñas

13. the war – la guerra
14. the guitar – la guitarra
15. the hat – el sombrero
16. the ducks – los patos
17. the point – el punto
18. the cows – las vacas
19. the teapot – la tetera
20. the eye – el ojo

PRACTICE EXERCISE 5

1. una cena
2. unos ojos
3. una trucha
4. unos patos
5. un punto
6. unas manzanas
7. una taza
8. una cigüeña
9. unos huevos
10. una naranja
11. un año
12. una vaca
13. unos quesos
14. unos zapatos
15. unas teteras
16. una rosa
17. unos sombreros
18. una bolsa
19. unas uñas
20. unas tazas

PRACTICE EXERCISE 6

1. some shoes – unos zapatos
2. an eye – un ojo
3. some cars – unos carros/coches
4. some gifts – unos regalos
5. a war – una guerra
6. a guitar – una guitarra
7. some courses – unos cursos
8. a cow – una vaca
9. some trouts – unas truchas
10. a hair – un pelo
11. some burps – unos eructos
12. a dinner – una cena
13. an orange – una naranja
14. some bags – unas bolsas
15. a year – un año
16. a fingernail – una uña
17. a teapot – una tetera
18. some ways – unos modos
19. a rose – una rosa
20. some ducks – unos patos

PRACTICE EXERCISE 7

1. unos cursos – los cursos
2. la tetera – una tetera
3. unos modos – los modos
4. las rosas – unas rosas
5. unos zapatos – los zapatos
6. un huevo – el huevo
7. las bolsas – unas bolsas

8. una planta – la planta
9. unos pingüinos – los pingüinos
10. la trucha – una trucha
11. unos carros – los carros
12. los regalos – unos regalos
13. una guerra – la guerra
14. los sombreros – unos sombreros
15. un ojo – el ojo

REVIEW EXERCISE 1

1. El pianista es Ramón.
2. Los violinistas son Felipe y Luis.
3. Los guitarristas son Claudia y Carlos.
4. La clarinetista es Teresa.
5. Las flautistas son Marta y Lucía.
6. Las pianistas son Carolina y Ester.
7. El violinista es Jorge.
8. La guitarrista es Carmen.
9. Las clarinetistas son Elena y Clara.
10. La flautista es Albita.

REVIEW EXERCISE 2

1. Ramón es un pianista.
2. Felipe y Luis son unos violinistas.
3. Claudia y Carlos son unos guitarristas.
4. Teresa es una clarinetista.
5. Paco y Roberto son unos flautistas.
6. Carolina y Juan son unos pianistas.
7. Jorge es un violinista.
8. Carmen es una guitarrista.

9. Elena y Clara son unas clarinetistas.

10. Albita es una flautista.

REVIEW EXERCISE 3

1. the (feminine-singular) – la

2. the (masculine-plural) – los

3. the (feminine-plural) – las

4. a or an (masculine-singular) – un

5. some (feminine-plural) – unas

6. shirt – camisa

7. hand – mano

8. shoulder – hombro

9. mouth – boca

10. spot – mancha

11. plate – plato

12. pianist – pianista

REVIEW EXERCISE 4

1. Manuel y Rafael son unos estudiantes españoles.

2. Silvia es una estudiante puertorriqueña.

3. Isabel y Beatriz son unas estudiantes cubanas.

4. Carlos es un estudiante mexicano.

5. Eduardo y Federico son unos estudiantes hondureños.

6. Alberto y Lisa son unos estudiantes argentinos.

7. Gabriela es una estudiante chilena.

8. Brenda y Luisa son unas estudiantes venezolanas.

9. Roberto y Beatriz son unos estudiantes panameños.

10. Ricardo es un estudiante costarricense.

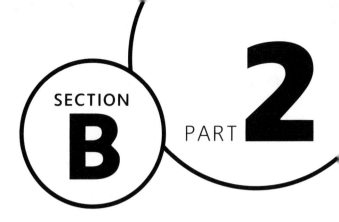

SECTION **B** PART **2**

Pronouns

Remember the definition of pronouns that you learned in elementary school? You don't need to be a pro to understand what a prounoun does in a sentence. Very simply, a pronoun is a word that replaces a noun. So, instead of saying "Neil Diamond" over and over again, you could just say "he." And instead of saying "his most wonderful song ever" over and over again, you could just say "it." That's a pronoun.

In this section we're going to learn the personal pronouns in Spanish. Pronouns, as we just saw, are very useful words, since they allow you to substitute the name of a person, place or thing with a shorter word. If it weren't for pronouns, there would be a lot of unnecessary repetition. Personal pronouns are pronouns for, well, people. The personal pronouns we'll learn in this section are the Spanish equivalent of *I, you, he, she, we,* and *they*. Personal pronouns are divided into first person, second person or third person pronouns. How do you distinguish between first, second or third person pronouns? The first person refers to the person who is talking. In English there are two first person pronouns: the singular pronoun *I* and the plural pronoun *we*. The second person refers to the person or persons that are being talked to. There is only one second person pronoun in English: *you*. The third person pronoun refers to someone else, the person being talked about. There are three third person personal pronouns in English: *he, she,* and *they.* In Spanish, there are more personal pronouns than there are in English. Once again, you need to pay attention to the gender of the person and the number (singular or plural) before determining which pronoun you'll use. To make things more complicated, you'll also need to determine the level of familiarity that you have with the person. But it's really not that hard. Let's look at the personal pronouns in Spanish in detail.

POINT 1: SECOND PERSON PRONOUNS

Okay, out of all the pronouns that we're going to learn, these are the most complicated. In Spanish there are several different ways of saying "you," whereas in English there is only one. As you know, the word "you" can be singular or plural. It refers to the people you're talking to, regardless of whether it is one person or a large group of people. Also, you may use the pronoun "you" when speaking to anyone, regardless of whether the person is young or old, friend or stranger, peer or superior. In Spanish, several different distinctions are made with the pronoun "you." You need to distinguish between singular and plural as well as between someone you know like a friend and someone you don't know well or to whom you need to show a little bit of respect. In addition to that, there are differences in usage between Spain and Latin America. There are five (yes, five!) different variations for the single English pronoun "you." Most beginner courses focus on the three forms that are used in Latin America and in Spain. We will discuss in detail how to use the first three forms, and we will explain briefly the other two forms that are only used in Spain.

TÚ (SINGULAR, FRIENDLY FORM OF "YOU")

The most common form of "you" is the pronoun *tú*. *Tú* is a singular pronoun that is used both in Spain and Latin America. You need to use *tú* when you're talking to a family member, a friend, a peer or someone who is your age. You would use *tú* with someone that you know fairly well or someone who is not a lot older than you. If you want to keep your job, make sure that you do not use *tú* when talking to your boss on your first day in the office! To summarize, *tú* is the singular form of "you" that refers to your equal, someone you know well, or someone who is younger than you.

USTED (SINGULAR, POLITE FORM OF "YOU")

The second pronoun that we need to learn is also used in both Spain and Latin America. *Usted* is a singular pronoun as well. The difference between *tú* and *usted* is that you use *usted* with someone who you don't know very well. You also use *usted* to refer to someone who is older than you or someone who holds a higher rank or position. You would use this with your boss, an older person or an adult that you don't know very well. You also need to use this form when you meet someone for the first time in a formal setting. It's safe to say that when in doubt, you should use *usted*. In written language, *usted* is often abbreviated as *Ud*. You notice that it's written with a capitalized *U* followed by the letter *d* and a period. However, when you write the complete word *usted*, you write it in lowercase unless it's at the beginning of a sentence. To recap, *usted* is the polite singular form of "you" that is used both in Spain and in Latin America.

USTEDES (PLURAL, ONLY FORM USED IN LATIN AMERICA, POLITE FORM IN SPAIN)

The next personal pronoun is used both in Latin America and in Spain. *Ustedes* is a plural personal pronoun, which means that you use it whenever you're speaking to a group of people. To make matters more complicated, there is a difference in the usage of *ustedes* between Spain and Latin America. In Spain, *ustedes* is considered to be a formal or polite pronoun. Spaniards would only use *ustedes* when talking to a group of people who are new acquaintances, older or higher in rank. In other words, they see *ustedes* as the plural form of *usted*. In Latin America, *ustedes* is used in any situation calling for a plural "you," regardless of age, rank or position. In other words, they see *ustedes* as the plural form of both *tú* and *usted*. *Ustedes* is often abbreviated by writing *Uds*. Again, we use lowercase when writing the complete form unless it's the first word of a sentence. Use a capital *U* followed by *ds* and a period when writing the abbreviation, regardless of whether it is at the beginning or in the middle of a sentence.

VOSOTROS (MASCULINE, PLURAL, FAMILIAR FORM OF "YOU," USED ONLY IN SPAIN)

This plural form of you is only used in Spain. As we mentioned earlier, in Spain and in Latin America a distinction is made between the familiar singular form of "you" (*tú*) and the polite singular form (*usted*). In Latin America there is only one plural form of "you" (*ustedes*) regardless of rank, age or familiarity. In Spain, a distinction is also made between familiar and polite in both the plural forms. You use the form *vosotros* whenever you're talking to a group of friends, peers or equals. Since it is a masculine pronoun, you use *vosotros* when talking to a group of male friends. You need to remember that in Spanish you use the masculine form when there is a mixed group of men and women. Therefore, you would use *vosotros* when talking to a group of male and female friends, even if there's only one man and ten women in the group.

VOSOTRAS (FEMININE, PLURAL, FAMILIAR FORM OF "YOU," USED ONLY IN SPAIN)

The feminine form of *vosotros* is *vosotras*. Again, this form is only used in Spain and not in Latin America. You use this form when talking to a group of women or girls that you know very well.

Vosotras is also a familiar form, therefore, you would not use it when talking to a group of women that you don't know very well, or women who are older or have a higher rank.

In case all this information is confusing, here's a summary chart of the second person Spanish pronouns that we've learned in this section:

tú	"You" – Singular – Familiar – Spain and Latin America
usted (Ud.)	"You" – Singular – Polite – Spain and Latin America
ustedes (Uds.)	"You" – Plural – Only plural form in Latin America – Polite form in Spain
vosotros	"You" – Plural – Masculine – Familiar form used only in Spain
vosotras	"You" – Plural – Feminine – Familiar form used only in Spain

PRACTICE EXERCISE 1

Match the following second person Spanish pronouns with their English equivalent.

1.	*usted*	"You" – singular – familiar form
2.	*vosotras*	Abbreviation of *ustedes*
3.	*Ud.*	"You" – plural used in Spain and Latin America
4.	*tú*	"You" – plural – masculine – used only in Spain
5.	*Uds.*	"You" – singular – polite form
6.	*vosotros*	"You" – plural – feminine – used only in Spain
7.	*ustedes*	Abbreviation of *usted*

PRACTICE EXERCISE 2

Say whether the following statements are True or False.

1. T F *Vosotros* is used in Spain and Latin America.
2. T F *Tú* is a plural form of you.
3. T F The plural form of "you" in Latin America is *ustedes*.
4. T F *Vosotros* can be used to refer to a group of both men and women in Spain.
5. T F The abbreviation of *usted* is Uds.
6. T F *Ustedes* is a plural form used in Latin America and in Spain.
7. T F In Spain there are three plural forms of "you": *ustedes*, *vosotros* and *vosotras*.
8. T F There are two plural forms of "you" in Latin America: *ustedes* and *vosotros*.
9. T F The abbreviation of *vosotros* is Uds.
10. T F *Tú* is used regardless of whether you're talking to a male or a female.

(**POINT 2:** FIRST PERSON PRONOUNS)

Okay, you can relax now, the most difficult part about pronouns is over. This is a very simple and straightforward section, since there are only three first person pronouns in Spanish. Luckily, you don't need to worry about different forms for Spain and Latin America. Before we get started, do you remember what first person pronouns are? The first person refers to the person or group of people doing the talking. If you're the only person talking, the personal pronoun is "I." If you're in a group of people, then the plural form of the first person is "we."

The Spanish pronoun for "I" is very easy to remember. If you're a rap artist, chances are you use the Spanish pronoun quite frequently. The Spanish word for "I" is *yo* as in "Wassup, yo!" You can imagine how some rap songs may sound to Spanish speakers who are unaware of the expression "yo!" To them it sounds like the pronoun "I" is being repeated throughout the song. "Wassup, I? Today I was on the subway, I, and this girl, I, she sat next to me, I and I, she kept looking at me, I . . . " You get the picture.

There's only one personal pronoun for the word "I." The Spanish personal pronoun *yo* is used regardless of whether you're a man or a woman. Remember the rules of capitalization that we learned earlier in the book? In English you always capitalize the pronoun "I." In Spanish you don't capitalize *yo* unless it is at the beginning of a sentence.

Now let's look at the plural cases. You need to look at gender when using the Spanish pronoun for "we." If you're a woman in a group of women, you would refer to yourselves as *nosotras*. *Nosotras* is the feminine form of "we." If you're a man in a group of men, you would refer to yourselves as *nosotros*. *Nosotros* is the masculine form of the pronoun "we." What we learned earlier about mixed groups of men and women applies here as well. If you're in a mixed group of men and women, you would refer to yourselves as *nosotros*.

So, here's a summary of the first person Spanish pronouns. There are three first person pronouns: *yo, nosotros* and *nosotras*. The only pronoun for "I" is *yo*. There are two Spanish pronouns that mean "we" in English. The masculine pronoun (which also includes a mixed group) is *nosotros*. The feminine pronoun for "we" is *nosotras*.

PRACTICE EXERCISE 3
Give the Spanish pronoun for each.

1. "We" – masculine form
2. "We" – feminine form
3. "I"
4. "You" – friendly, singular
5. "You" – polite, singular
6. "You" – only plural form used in Latin America, also used in Spain as a polite form
7. "You" – plural, masculine, familiar, used only in Spain
8. "You" – plural, feminine, familiar, used only in Spain
9. Abbreviated form of #5 above
10. Abbreviated form of #6 above

(**POINT 3:** THIRD PERSON PRONOUNS)

The third person personal pronouns in English are "he," "she" and "they." "He" and "she" are singular pronouns and "they" is a plural pronoun. In Spanish, there are four third person pronouns. As it happened with the second person pronouns, there is no distinction in the third person between Spain and Latin America. Let's look at the third person pronouns in detail.

The Spanish word for "he" is *él*. Notice that there's an accent mark on the *e*. That is because we need to distinguish between the masculine definite article *el*, which as you know means "the," and the pronoun *él*, which means "he." This is another case in which the accent mark changes the meaning of a word. The accent mark is very important because otherwise people would not know whether you're writing "he" or "the." However, keep in mind that there is no difference in pronunciation between the word *él* (he) and *el* (the).

The Spanish word for "she" is *ella*. This personal pronoun doesn't have an accent mark. Remember the rules of pronunciation for the sound of the double LL? The sound of the double LL in Spanish is similar to the sound of the letter "y" in English. You don't want to pronounce *ella* the way you say the name of the singer Ella Fitzgerald, instead you pronounce it as "eh-yah."

There are two pronouns in Spanish that mean "they." One of the pronouns is masculine and the other is feminine. The masculine plural third person pronoun is *ellos*. Also remember that in Spanish we use the masculine form to refer to a group of people of both sexes. To refer to a group of men or a mixed group of men and women, you use the pronoun *ellos*. The feminine plural third person pronoun is *ellas*. You would use this pronoun to refer to a group of women.

PRACTICE EXERCISE 4

Write the appropriate third person pronoun (*él, ella, ellos* or *ellas*) that corresponds to each person or group of people.

1. *Carlos*
2. *Carlos y Roberto*
3. *María y Julia*
4. *Julio y Julia*

5. *Julio, Roberto y Julia*

6. *Julia*

7. *Julio*

8. *Julia, María y Roberta*

POINT 4: REVIEW

Let's review all the personal pronouns that we've learned in this section.

Yo is the Spanish word for "I."

Tú is the singular familiar way of saying "you." It's used with people that you know well or with people who are younger than you.

Usted is the singular polite way of saying "you." It's used with people who are older than you, people that you don't know very well, or people in a higher position.

Él is the word for "he." Remember to use an accent mark, otherwise you're writing the definite article "the."

Ella is the word for "she." Remember to pronounce it like this: "eh-yah"

Nosotros is one of the words that means "we." It's a masculine word but it should also be used with mixed groups.

Nosotras also means "we." It's a feminine word.

Ellos is one of the words that means "they." It's a masculine word that should also be used with mixed groups.

Ellas also means "they." It's a feminine word.

Ustedes is a plural form of "you." It's the only plural form used in Latin America. In Spain, this form is only used as a polite way of saying "you" in plural.

Vosotros is a plural form of "you." It's only used in Spain. It's a familiar masculine form.

Vosotras is another plural form of "you." It's only used in Spain. It's the female version of *vosotros*.

(NOW, WATCH THE DVD)

If you've digested this information, turn on your DVD and watch Section 9.

REVIEW EXERCISES
Now that you've gone through the section in the book, and then watched it on the DVD, here's another chance to practice what you've learned.

REVIEW EXERCISE 1
Match the following pronouns with their English equivalent.

1. *nosotros*   Abbreviation of *usted*
2. *ella*   "They" – masculine form
3. *usted*   "You" – singular, familiar form
4. *él*   "You" – singular polite form
5. *yo*   "We" – masculine form

6. *tú*   "He"
7. *ustedes*   Abbreviation of *ustedes*
8. *ellas*   "I"
9. *vosotros*   "She"
10. *Uds.*   "You" – plural, familiar, masculine form, used only in Spain
11. *nosotras*   "You" – plural, used both in Latin America and Spain
12. *ellos*   "They" – feminine form
13. *Ud.*   "You" – plural, familiar, feminine form, used only in Spain
14. *vosotras*   "We" – feminine form

REVIEW EXERCISE 2

Write the appropriate pronoun that corresponds to each person or group of people.

1. Teresa
2. Teresa and Susana
3. Carlos
4. María and Luis
5. Roberto and Pablo
6. Roberto, Pablo and I
7. You (my best friend)
8. You (I've just met you)
9. You (Paco and Alberto, in Latin America)
10. You (Paco and Alberto, in Spain)

REVIEW EXERCISE 3

Say whether the following statements are True or False.

1. T F *Yo* is the Spanish word for "you."
2. T F *Tú* is the singular familiar way of saying "you."
3. T F *Usted* is the plural polite way of saying "you."
4. T F *Él* is the word for "she."
5. T F *Ella* is the word for "he."
6. T F *Nosotros* is the masculine word that means "we."
7. T F *Nosotras* also means "we." It's a feminine word.
8. T F *Ellos* is one of the words that means "you."
9. T F *Ellas* is a feminine word that means "they."
10. T F *Ustedes* is a plural form of "you."
11. T F *Vosotros* is a plural form of "you" that is used only in Spain.
12. T F *Vosotras* is the female version of *nosotros*.

REVIEW EXERCISE 4

Translate the following English words into Spanish.

1. he
2. she
3. they (masculine)
4. you (singular, familiar)
5. they (feminine)
6. you (singular, polite)
7. you (plural, used in Spain and Latin America)
8. we (masculine)

Answer Key

PRACTICE EXERCISE 1

1. usted – "You" – singular – polite form
2. vosotras – "You" – plural – feminine – used only in Spain
3. Ud. – Abbreviation of usted
4. tú – "You" – singular – familiar form
5. Uds. – Abbreviation of ustedes
6. vosotros – "You" – plural – masculine – used only in Spain
7. ustedes – "You" – plural used in Spain and Latin America

PRACTICE EXERCISE 2

1. FALSE
2. FALSE
3. TRUE
4. TRUE

5. FALSE

6. TRUE

7. TRUE

8. FALSE

9. FALSE

10. TRUE

PRACTICE EXERCISE 3

1. nosotros

2. nosotras

3. yo

4. tú

5. usted

6. ustedes

7. vosotros

8. vosotras

9. Ud.

10. Uds.

PRACTICE EXERCISE 4

1. él

2. ellos

3. ellas

4. ellos

5. ellos

6. ella

7. él

8. ellas

REVIEW EXERCISE 1

1. nosotros – We – masculine form
2. ella – She
3. usted – You – singular polite form
4. él – He
5. yo – I
6. tú – You – singular, familiar form
7. ustedes – You – plural, used both in Latin America and Spain
8. ellas – They – feminine form
9. vosotros – You – plural, familiar, masculine form, used only in Spain
10. Uds. – Abbreviation of ustedes
11. nosotras – We – feminine form
12. ellos – They – masculine form
13. Ud. – Abbreviation of usted
14. vosotras – You – plural, familiar, feminine form, used only in Spain

REVIEW EXERCISE 2

1. ella
2. ellas
3. él
4. ellos
5. ellos
6. nosotros
7. tú
8. usted
9. ustedes
10. vosotros

REVIEW EXERCISE 3

1. FALSE
2. TRUE
3. FALSE
4. FALSE
5. FALSE
6. TRUE
7. TRUE
8. FALSE
9. TRUE
10. TRUE
11. TRUE
12. FALSE

REVIEW EXERCISE 4

1. él
2. ella
3. ellos
4. tú
5. ellas
6. usted
7. ustedes
8. nosotros

The Verbs Ser *and* Estar

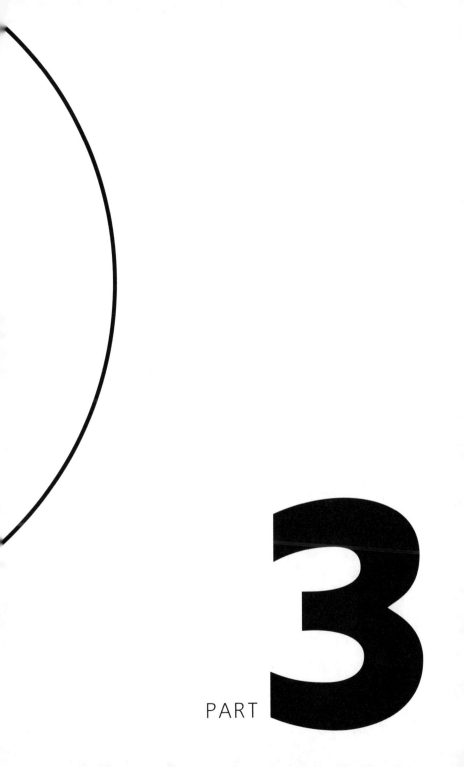

PART **3**

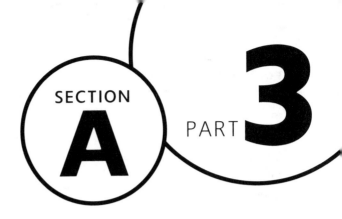

The Verb **Ser**

In Spanish, there are two verbs that mean "to be."
One is the verb *ser* and the other is the verb *estar*.
There are certain conditions that call for the verb
ser rather than the verb *estar*. It's not very difficult;
you'll soon get a feel for when to use each verb. In
this section we're going to focus on the verb *ser*.
But before we start, let's look at some new
vocabulary.

lo siento – I'm sorry

perro – dog

bonito – pretty

sillas – chairs

guapo – handsome

hija – daughter

desordenado – slob

caballo – horse

horrible – horrible

panadería – bakery

galletas – cookies

gratis – free

actor – actor

turista – tourist

alumno – student

farmacéutico – pharmacist

profesor – professor

simpático – nice

alto – tall

bajo – short

feo – ugly

delgado – thin

gordo – fat

rubio – blond

antipático – mean, unfriendly

inteligente – smart

PRACTICE EXERCISE 1

Match the Spanish word in the left column with the English word in the right column.

1. *caballo*   slob
2. *feo*   cookies
3. *sillas*   bakery
4. *hija*   actor
5. *panadería*   horrible
6. *rubio*   I'm sorry.
7. *turista*   tall
8. *desordenado*   chairs
9. *alumno*   blond
10. *actor*   short
11. *horrible*   horse
12. *Lo siento.*   student
13. *galletas*   daughter
14. *alto*   tourist
15. *bajo*   ugly

PRACTICE EXERCISE 2

Fill in the blanks with the correct Spanish word.

1. He's mean, the opposite of *simpático:* __ __ t __ p á __ __ __ __.
2. The opposite of *guapo* is __ e __.
3. Some people think Arnold Schwarzenegger is
   un __ c __ __ __ __   h __ rr __ __ __ __ __.
4. The Spanish word for horse is c __ __ __ __ __ __.
5. The opposite of *delgado* is __ __ r __ __.

6. I love the smell of freshly baked __ a __ __ e __ __ s.
7. I need to buy bread in the p__ n__ d __ __ __ a.
8. It's better than cheap, it's __ r __ __ i __.

POINT 2: WHEN TO USE THE VERB *SER*

We mentioned earlier that there are two different verbs in Spanish that mean "to be." The first of those verbs is the verb *ser* and the second one is *estar*. The main difference between the two verbs is that the verb *ser* usually refers to a permanent condition, whereas the verb *estar* refers to a variable or temporary condition.

Now that you know the different pronouns, we'll show you the various forms of the verb *ser* that go along with each pronoun. This is what we call "conjugating" a verb. In Spanish, just like in English, all verbs are conjugated. In other words, we take the base form of a verb and we change it according to the subject of that verb. English conjugations are simple – just add "-s" to the "he," "she," or "it" form. "I see" becomes "he sees." Spanish conjugations are a bit more complex, but luckily most verbs in Spanish are conjugated in a predictable way. However, *ser* is what's called an "irregular" verb, because it's not conjugated in a predictable way; you just have to memorize it. Most beginner students hate irregular verbs because they need to be memorized individually. But you can relax, as we said earlier, most of the Spanish verbs are regular and pretty easy to deal with.

Let's look at the conjugation of the verb "to be" in English (which, by the way, is also irregular!) so that you can see what a conjugation looks like. Then we'll conjugate the verb *ser*. The English conjugation of "to be" is:

TO BE

I	am	We	are
You	are	You (plural)	are
He/She	is	They	are

And the conjugation of the verb *ser* is:

SER

Yo	soy	Nosotros/Nosotras	somos
Tú	eres	Vosotros/Vosotras	sois*
Él		Ellos	
Ella	es	Ellas	son
Usted		Ustedes	

*As we mentioned earlier, the vosotros/vosotras form is used only in Spain. Most beginner courses focus only on the second person plural Ustedes, which is used both in Spain and Latin America. We're showing you the vosotros/vosotras form for informational purposes only. Maybe you're going to Spain, after all!

You notice that each subject pronoun has a corresponding conjugated verb. But what happens when instead of a pronoun you have a noun? In that case you would use the conjugated form that would correspond to the noun if it were replaced by a pronoun. For example, if the subject of the sentence is *Roberto*, you would have to use *es* because *Roberto* is the same as "he" or *él*. If the subject of the sentence is *Roberto y María* (Robert and Mary), you would have to use *son* because *Roberto and María* is the same as "they" or *ellos*. Simple, right?

Okay, so what happens if the subject of the sentence is a combination of two or more pronouns? In that case, you would have to consider both pronouns <u>combined</u> before deciding which conjugated form you'll use. For example, let's consider the combined subject *Tú y yo* or "You and I." We know that the conjugated form of *ser* for the pronoun *tú* is *eres* and that the conjugated form for the pronoun *yo* is *soy*. But that's only if you consider the pronouns individually. You need to consider both pronouns <u>combined</u> before deciding the form you'll use. "You and I" combined is the same as "we." That's why in this case you would use the form *somos*, the conjugated form of *ser* for the pronoun *nosotros*.

Ready for a challenge? Can you guess the form that you would use for *él y ella*? If your answer is *son* you can pat yourself on the back. Let's analyze this: "he" + "she" = "they" (*él* + *ella* = *ellos*), therefore you need to use the conjugated form for *ellos*, or *son*. How about *ella y tú*? Let's see, "she" + "you" = plural "you" (*ella* + *tú* = *ustedes*); therefore, you need to use the conjugated form for "you" in plural, or *ustedes – son.* (Or *vosotros sois* in Spain!)

Now let's talk about when you need to use the verb *ser.* As we mentioned earlier, *ser* is used for permanent or relatively permanent situations. In Spanish, you use the verb *ser* when talking about a person's physical description (short, fat), personality traits (nice, smart), occupation or place of origin. Yes, I know what you're thinking . . . That being nice, smart or thin is not permanent. It's true, people change occupations, gain weight, become dumber or meaner during their lifetime, but these are things that are considered to be relatively permanent because it takes a long time to change. Strangely, you would have to use the verb *ser* to say that someone is a tourist. This is one exception to the rule since being a tourist is normally a transitory situation! Yes, I'm sure that you've met people who seem to go through life as eternal tourists, but that's not the case for most of us, who have to go back to school, to our jobs, etc. So, to express that someone is a tourist, use the verb *ser* even if it seems a bit illogical.

Now let's look at the following example and analyze what each word does in the sentence:

Yo soy de Chile. (I am from Chile.)

▶ *Yo* is the subject of the sentence; it's a pronoun that means "I."
▶ *Soy* is the conjugated form of *ser* that goes along with *yo.*
▶ *De* is the preposition "from."
▶ *Chile* is the name of the country.

Let's look at other examples:

Soy de Panamá. (I am from Panama.)

Notice that the sentence begins with the verb *soy*. We're not talking about soy milk here, but the conjugated form of the verb *ser*. We decided not to use a pronoun in this sentence. That's because it's not really needed. In many sentences in Spanish, the subject may be left out and the sentence still makes perfect sense. That is because *soy* implies the subject *yo* or "I." You see, there's no other pronoun that goes with the conjugated verb *soy*. In other words, *soy* can't be used with *tú, él, ella, usted, nosotros, nosotras, ellos, ellas* or *ustedes*. The only subject pronoun that is used with *soy* is *yo*. That's why you may want to leave out the subject in many sentences in Spanish. In most sentences, the conjugated verb implies the subject of the sentence. As we said earlier, it's not required that you leave out the subject, it's really up to you.

Ella es de California. (She's from California.)

Notice how in this case we did not leave out the pronoun. That's because *es* can be used with *él, ella* and *usted*. The person that you're talking to may not know if you're referring to the subject "he," "she" or "you." Not including the subject in this sentence would be ambiguous unless the person already knew whom you were talking about.

Somos de Costa Rica. (We're from Costa Rica.)

Notice how there's no pronoun in this sentence. We decided to leave it out because the conjugated verb *somos* is only used with the pronoun "we" (*nosotros/nosotras*).

We've been looking at examples where we express where a person is from. But remember, *ser* is not used only to talk about origin or nationalities. You should use *ser* to describe other permanent or relatively permanent characteristics of a person, place or thing. As we said earlier, you use the verb *ser* to talk about physical descriptions (of a person, place or thing), personality traits or occupations.

Notice the following sentence:

El gato es bonito. (The cat is pretty.)

▶ *El* is the definite article "the." We use the masculine article because it has to match the masculine noun, *gato*. Notice that it doesn't carry an accent, otherwise it would mean "he."
▶ *Gato* is the masculine noun that means "cat."
▶ *Es* is the conjugated form of *ser* that goes with the third person singular subject.
▶ *Bonito* is a masculine adjective that describes the cat as pretty.

Now let's look at the same sentence in the feminine form.

La gata es bonita. (The female cat is pretty.)

▶ *La* is the definite article "the." We use the feminine article because it has to match the feminine noun, *gata* or female cat.

▶ *Gata* is the feminine form of *gato*, notice how we changed the *o* into an *a*.

▶ *Es* is the conjugated form of *ser* that goes with the third person singular subject.

▶ *Bonita* is the feminine form of the adjective *bonito*. In Spanish, the gender of the adjective has to change to describe a feminine noun or pronoun. Notice how the adjective gets an *a* at the end in order to modify a feminine subject.

Now let's look at a sentence with a plural subject.

Los profesores son feos. (The professors are ugly.)

▶ *Los* is the definite article "the." Notice that we chose the masculine plural article. That's because it modifies a masculine plural noun: *profesores*.

▶ *Profesores* is the plural form of the masculine noun *profesor*.

▶ *Son* is the conjugated form of the verb *ser* that goes with the third person plural pronouns *ellos, ellas* and *ustedes*.

▶ *Feos* is the masculine plural form of the adjective *feo*, and it agrees with *profesores*.

Making these sentences is like a puzzle. The conjugated verb has to match the subject of the sentence. The adjective and definite article need to match in gender and number the noun that they are modifying. If all pieces of the puzzle fit, you've created a grammatically correct sentence. Congratulations! ¡Felicitaciones!

PRACTICE EXERCISE 3

The following people have different occupations. Write the correct form of the verb *ser* to complete each sentence. Don't forget that *y* is the Spanish word for "and."

1. *El señor Rodríguez _____ profesor.*
2. *Nosotros _____ alumnos.*
3. *Rosa y Raúl _____ abogados.*
4. *Ella _____ farmacéutica.*
5. *María y yo _____ alumnos.*
6. *Meryl Streep y Jack Nicholson _____ actores.*
7. *Tú _____ piloto.*
8. *Usted _____ profesor.*
9. *Roberto, María y yo _____ alumnos.*
10. *Yo _____ dentista.*

PRACTICE EXERCISE 4

The following people have different nationalities. Write the correct form of the verb *ser* to finish each sentence. Don't forget that *y* is the Spanish word for "and." Also, remember that in Spanish the adjectives that express nationalities are not capitalized.

1. *Tú _____ colombiano.*
2. *Ella _____ nicaragüense.*
3. *Nereyda y Guadalupe _____ mexicanas.*

4. Víctor _____ puertorriqueño.
5. Ustedes _____ chilenos.
6. Nosotros _____ americanos.
7. Usted _____ argentino.
8. Yo _____ ecuatoriano.
9. Pepe y yo _____ costarricenses.
10. Roberto y tú _____ panameños.

PRACTICE EXERCISE 5

The following people have different physical characteristics and personalities. Complete each sentence with the correct form of *ser*.

1. Usted _____ bajo.
2. Ella _____ fea.
3. Él _____ inteligente.
4. Nosotras _____ delgadas.
5. Los caballos _____ rápidos.
6. Los perros _____ antipáticos.
7. El gato _____ bonito.
8. La gata _____ bonita.
9. El perro y el gato _____ gordos.
10. Tú _____ desordenado.
11. Yo _____ guapo.
12. Ustedes _____ altos.
13. Tú y yo _____ inteligentes.
14. Él y tú _____ gordos.
15. Ella y él _____ horribles.

NOW, WATCH THE DVD

If you've digested this information, turn on your DVD and watch Sections 11 and 12.

REVIEW EXERCISES
Now that you've gone through the section in the book, and then watched it on the DVD, here's a chance to show what you know.

REVIEW EXERCISE 1
Give the Spanish translation of each of the following words or phrases.

1. I'm sorry.
2. dog
3. pretty
4. chairs
5. blond
6. handsome
7. daughter
8. slob
9. horse
10. horrible
11. bakery
12. cookies
13. free
14. actor
15. student
16. nice
17. ugly

18. thin
19. fat
20. smart

REVIEW EXERCISE 2

Fill in the appropriate forms of the verb *ser*.

1. *yo* _____
2. *tú* _____
3. *ellos* _____
4. *nosotros* _____
5. *ellas* _____
6. *él* _____
7. *usted* _____
8. *ustedes* _____

REVIEW EXERCISE 3

Now complete each sentence with the correct form of the verb *ser*.

1. *Yo* _____ *dominicano.*
2. *Ella* _____ *peruana.*
3. *Ellas* _____ *cubanas.*
4. *Carlos* _____ *hondureño.*
5. *El caballo* _____ *venezolano.*
6. *Nosotros* _____ *salvadoreños.*
7. *Pedro y Julio* _____ *canadienses.*
8. *Él y ella* _____ *uruguayos.*
9. *Tú* _____ *boliviano.*
10. *Usted* _____ *colombiano.*

REVIEW EXERCISE 4

Let's try that again! Write the correct form of the verb *ser* in each sentence.

1. *Él* _____ *profesor.*
2. *Ellos* _____ *guapos.*
3. *Ellas* _____ *alumnas.*
4. *Tú* _____ *inteligente.*
5. *Rosa* _____ *abogada.*
6. *Tú y yo* _____ *desordenados.*
7. *Marta y Lola* _____ *farmacéuticas.*
8. *Nosotros* _____ *alumnos.*
9. *Usted* _____ *alto.*
10. *Johnny Depp y Gwyneth Paltrow* _____ *actores.*
11. *Marcos y Mateo* _____ *pilotos.*
12. *Usted* _____ *profesor.*
13. *Él y tú* _____ *inteligentes.*
14. *Tú y yo* _____ *alumnos.*
15. *Ustedes* _____ *dentistas.*
16. *Rebeca* _____ *baja.*
17. *La perra* _____ *fea.*
18. *Él* _____ *inteligente.*
19. *El perro y el gato* _____ *rápidos.*
20. *Nosotras* _____ *simpáticas.*

Answer Key

PRACTICE EXERCISE 1

1. caballo – horse
2. feo – ugly
3. sillas – chairs
4. hija – daughter
5. panadería – bakery
6. rubio – blond
7. turista – tourist
8. desordenado – slob
9. alumno – student
10. actor – actor
11. horrible – horrible
12. Lo siento. – I'm sorry.
13. galletas – cookies
14. alto – tall
15. bajo – short

PRACTICE EXERCISE 2

1. He's mean, the opposite of simpático: antipático.
2. The opposite of guapo is feo.
3. Arnold Schwarzenegger is un actor horrible.
4. The Spanish word for horse is caballo.
5. The opposite of delgado is gordo.
6. I love the smell of freshly baked galletas.
7. I need to buy bread in the panadería
8. It's better than cheap, it's gratis.

PRACTICE EXERCISE 3

1. El Señor Rodríguez es profesor.
2. Nosotros somos alumnos.
3. Rosa y Raúl son abogados.
4. Ella es farmacéutica.
5. María y yo somos alumnos.
6. Meryl Streep y Jack Nicholson son actores.
7. Tú eres piloto.
8. Usted es profesor.
9. Roberto, María y yo somos alumnos.
10. Yo soy dentista.

PRACTICE EXERCISE 4

1. Tú eres colombiano.
2. Ella es nicaragüense.
3. Nereyda y Guadalupe son mexicanas.
4. Víctor es puertorriqueño.
5. Ustedes son chilenos.
6. Nosotros somos americanos.
7. Usted es argentino.

8. Yo soy ecuatoriano.

9. Pepe y yo somos costarricenses.

10. Roberto y tú son panameños. (Or sois in Spain.)

PRACTICE EXERCISE 5

1. Usted es bajo.

2. Ella es fea.

3. Él es inteligente.

4. Nosotras somos delgadas.

5. Los caballos son rápidos.

6. Los perros son antipáticos.

7. El gato es bonito.

8. La gata es bonita.

9. El perro y el gato son gordos.

10. Tú eres desordenado.

11. Yo soy guapo.

12. Ustedes son altos.

13. Tú y yo somos inteligentes.

14. Él y tú son gordos. (Or sois)

15. Ella y él son horribles.

REVIEW EXERCISE 1

1. I'm sorry. – Lo siento.

2. dog – perro

3. pretty – bonito, bonita

4. chairs – sillas

5. blond – rubio

6. handsome – guapo

7. daughter – hija

8. slob – desordenado

9. horse – caballo
10. horrible – horrible
11. bakery – panadería
12. cookies – galletas
13. free – gratis
14. actor – actor
15. student – alumno
16. nice – simpático
17. ugly – feo
18. thin – delgado
19. fat – gordo
20. smart – inteligente

REVIEW EXERCISE 2

1. soy
2. eres
3. son
4. somos
5. son
6. es
7. es
8. son

REVIEW EXERCISE 3

1. Yo soy dominicano.
2. Ella es peruana.
3. Ellas son cubanas.
4. Carlos es hondureño.
5. El caballo es venezolano.
6. Nosotros somos salvadoreños.

7. Pedro y Julio son canadienses.

8. Él y ella son uruguayos.

9. Tú eres boliviano.

10. Usted es colombiano.

REVIEW EXERCISE 4

1. Él es profesor.

2. Ellos son guapos.

3. Ellas son alumnas.

4. Tú eres inteligente.

5. Rosa es abogada.

6. Tú y yo somos desordenados.

7. Marta y Lola son farmacéuticas.

8. Nosotros somos alumnos.

9. Usted es alto.

10. Johnny Depp y Gwyneth Paltrow son actores.

11. Marcos y Mateo son pilotos.

12. Usted es profesor.

13. Él y tú son inteligentes. (Or sois)

14. Tú y yo somos alumnos.

15. Ustedes son dentistas.

16. Rebeca es baja.

17. La perra es fea.

18. Él es inteligente.

19. El perro y el gato son rápidos.

20. Nosotras somos simpáticas.

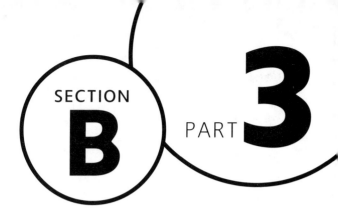

SECTION **B** PART **3**

The Verb Estar

Now that you've learned the verb *ser* you're ready to learn the second Spanish verb that means "to be." But before we explain the verb *estar* in detail, let's look at some new vocabulary.

cansado – tired

el loco – the fool, the crazy person

pollo – chicken

cocina – kitchen

la luna – the moon

feliz – happy

triste – sad

confundido – confused

loco – crazy

teatro – theater

hospital – hospital

aeropuerto – airport

museo – museum

escuela – school

farmacia – pharmacy

playa – beach

universidad – university

sala – living room

enfermo – sick

preocupado – worried

ahora – now

PRACTICE EXERCISE 1

Match the Spanish word in the left column with the English word in the right column.

1. *preocupado*   sad
2. *enfermo*   museum

3.	*cansado*	chicken
4.	*feliz*	crazy
5.	*triste*	beach
6.	*confundido*	airport
7.	*escuela*	sick
8.	*museo*	kitchen
9.	*aeropuerto*	tired
10.	*farmacia*	worried
11.	*hospital*	school
12.	*playa*	hospital
13.	*pollo*	confused
14.	*cocina*	happy
15.	*loco*	pharmacy

PRACTICE EXERCISE 2

Fill in the blanks with the correct Spanish word.

1. You would find many airplanes at an *a __ r __ __ u __ r __ o.*
2. The room in the house where you're likely to make *galletas* is the *c __ c __ __ __ __.*
3. You buy your medicines in a *__ a __ m __ __ __ __ a.*
4. She was *triste* before, but now she's *__ e __ __ z.*
5. In the *cocina* you can make fried *__ __ ll __.*
6. She seems to be very *__ __ n __ __ n __ __ d __,* she doesn't know what to do.
7. He was so *enfermo* that he was admitted in the *__ __ s __ __ t __ __.*
8. They have a wonderful Picasso in that *__ __ s __ __.*
9. In the summer, I like to spend the weekend in the *__ __ a __ __.*
10. He slept ten hours, he's no longer *__ a __ s __ __ __.*

POINT 2: WHEN TO USE THE VERB *ESTAR*

As we said earlier, the verb "to be" has two different forms in Spanish. In the previous section we learned that the verb *ser* is used whenever we want to express a condition or situation that is permanent or not very likely to change. The verb *estar* also means "to be," but it is used to express situations that are temporary or likely to change. We'll have more on that soon, but first let's look at the conjugation of the verb.

As you study the conjugation of the verb *estar*, notice that it's the last part of the verb (the –ar) that changes. The root or stem of the verb (the *est–* part) remains the same. *Estar* falls under the category of –ar verbs. As you will see in the future, most Spanish verbs fall under this category. Regular –ar verbs follow the same pattern of conjugation; they will drop their –ar endings and add the same new endings in the same places. Now let's look at how *estar* is conjugated.

ESTAR

Yo	**estoy**	Nosotros/ Nosotras	**estamos**
Tú	**estás**	Vosotros/ Vosotras	**estáis**
Él		Ellos	
Ella	**está**	Ellas	**están**
Usted		Ustedes	

You may have noticed that there are accent marks on *estás, está, estáis* and *están*. Unless you want to get a lot of red marks on your test papers, make sure to include the accent marks when writing these verbs. That's because not putting the accent mark on a word may change the meaning of the word. For example, the word *esta* without the accent mark means "this," whereas the word *está* with the accent mark is the conjugated form of the verb *estar*. So, consider yourselves warned, make sure you write those accent marks!

So, when do you use the verb *estar*? As we mentioned earlier, you use this verb when describing characteristics of a person, place or thing that are likely to change. You need to use the verb *estar* to describe how a person is feeling at the moment. You would also use it to express the momentary location of a person, place or thing.

Let's look at the following example and analyze what each word does in the sentence:

Yo estoy cansado. (I am tired.)

▶ *Yo* is the subject of the sentence, it's the pronoun that means "I."
▶ *Estoy* is the conjugated form of *estar* that goes along with *yo*.
▶ *Cansado* is the masculine adjective that means "tired." If you're a woman you need to say *Yo estoy cansada*.

Why did we use the verb *estar* and not the verb *ser*? Being tired is a temporary state that doesn't describe your personality. You would never use the verb *ser* with *cansado*, because it would mean that you're a tired person who is going to be always, forever, permanently tired. So, use the verb *estar* unless you want to express that you'll be tired for the rest of your life! And start getting some serious sleep, will you?

Let's take a look at another example:

Estoy en la cocina. (I'm in the kitchen.)

▶ *Estoy* is the conjugated form of the verb *estar* that corresponds to *yo*. The pronoun has been omitted because *estoy* only matches one subject, the pronoun *yo*. By looking at the conjugated verb the person you're talking to knows that the subject is *yo*.
▶ *En* is the preposition "in."
▶ *La* is the definite article "the." We use a feminine article because it's modifying the feminine word *cocina*.
▶ *Cocina* is the feminine noun that means "kitchen."

And why did we decide to use the verb *estar* instead of *ser*? Expressing location is another condition that calls for the verb *estar*. It's easy to understand why. The location of a person, place or thing changes easily. We're not talking about the origin or nationality of a person, which is relatively permanent, but rather the momentary location. In other words, you may be working hard in your *cocina* making your fried *pollo* when the *teléfono* rings and you go to the *sala* to answer your friend Rosario's call. In a matter of seconds your location has changed. When you were in the kitchen you may have said *Estoy en la cocina,* and after moving to the living room *Estoy en la sala.*

Also, notice how in these two examples the personal pronoun *yo* was omitted. This is something optional that you can do in Spanish. That's because the conjugated verb *estoy* only matches the subject *yo*. When you say *estoy* the subject *yo* is clearly implied. You would not be able to omit the pronoun and be understood clearly with the conjugated form *está*. That's because the conjugated form *está* matches three pronouns: *él, ella* and *usted*.

Now, here's a summary of the different uses of the verb *SER* and *ESTAR*:

SER

SER means "to be". It's used to express conditions that are permanent or unlikely to change easily. It can be used with expressions indicating:	
1. Nationalities or places of origin:	Yo **soy** de los Estados Unidos. (I'm from the U.S.)
	Gloria **es** colombiana. (Gloria is Colombian.)
2. Professions or occupations:	Roberto y Raúl **son** dentistas. (R. and R. are dentists.)
	Usted **es** profesor. (You are a professor.)
3. Basic characteristics:	Nosotros **somos** guapos. (We are handsome.)
	Ella **es** fea. (She is ugly.)

ESTAR

ESTAR also means "to be". It's used to express transitory conditions that are likely to change easily. It expresses where the subject is and how the subject feels. It indicates:

1. Location:	*Lola* **está** *en el museo.* (Lola is in the museum.)
	El perro y el gato **están** *en la cocina.* (The dog and the cart are in the kitchen.)
2. Feelings or conditions that change:	*Ellas* **están** *confundidas.* (They are confused.)
	Yo **estoy** *feliz.* (I am happy.)

PRACTICE EXERCISE 3

Fill in each blank with the appropriate form of the verb *estar* in the following sentences expressing locations.

1. *El farmacéutico* _____ *en la farmacia.*
2. *Los turistas* _____ *en el museo.*
3. *María y Ana* _____ *en el hospital.*
4. *Los gatos* _____ *en la sala.*
5. *Nosotros* _____ *en la universidad.*
6. *Tú y yo* _____ *en el cine.*

7. Usted _____ en el teatro.
8. El señor _____ en el carro.
9. Ustedes _____ en el ferrocarril.
10. Pepa y tú _____ en la cocina.

PRACTICE EXERCISE 4

Fill in each blank with the appropriate form of *estar* in the following sentences expressing feelings.

1. Nosotros _____ enfermos.
2. Yo _____ feliz.
3. Tú _____ preocupado.
4. Clara y Jesús _____ tristes.
5. Enrique y Kevin _____ confundidos.
6. Juan y yo _____ cansados.
7. Ustedes _____ locos.
8. Usted _____ bien.
9. Ana María _____ feliz.
10. Las hormigas _____ confundidas.

(NOW, WATCH THE DVD)

If you've digested this information, turn on your DVD and watch Section 13.

REVIEW EXERCISES

Now that you've gone through the section in the book, and then watched it on the DVD, here's a chance to show what you know.

REVIEW EXERCISE 1

Determine whether you need to use *ser* or *estar* and circle the correct form.

1. *Juan (es / está) triste.*
2. *Las manzanas (son / están) rojas* (red).
3. *Nosotros (somos / estamos) en California.*
4. *Nosotros (somos / estamos) de California.*
5. *Cinco más* (plus) *uno (es / está) seis.*
6. *Yo (soy / estoy) enfermo.*
7. *Ellas (son / están) inteligentes.*
8. *La mesa (es / está) en la cocina.*
9. *La mesa (es / está) italiana.*
10. *El café (es / está) colombiano.*
11. *¡Hola! ¿Cómo (eres / estás)?*
12. *Los taxis (son / están) ocupados* (occupied).
13. *Julia y Juan (son / están) altos.*
14. *Usted (es / está) feliz.*
15. *La muchacha (es / está) bonita.*

REVIEW EXERCISE 2

Fill in each blank with the appropriate conjugated form of either *SER* or *ESTAR*.

1. *Pedro _____ piloto. Él _____ en el aeropuerto.*
2. *Elena _____ en la escuela. Ella _____ estudiante.*
3. *Nosotros _____ turistas. Nosotros _____ en el café.*

4. Usted _____ en el hospital. Usted _____ doctor.

5. Silvia y Ricardo _____ actores. Ellos _____ en el teatro.

6. El señor Martínez _____ en la farmacia. Él _____ farmacéutico.

7. Rafael y Federico _____ aficionados (fans). Ellos _____ en el concierto (concert).

8. Ustedes _____ alpinistas (mountain climbers). Ustedes _____ en la montaña (mountain).

9. Yo _____ en el parque (park). Yo _____ turista.

10. Laura y Viviana _____ buenas bailarinas (good dancers). Ellas _____ en la discoteca (dance club).

REVIEW EXERCISE 3

Translate the following sentences into Spanish.

1. I'm tired.
2. We're students.
3. They (masculine) are from the United States.
4. She's short.
5. You (polite) are happy.
6. You (familiar) and I are writers.
7. You (polite) are tall.
8. You (plural) are dentists.
9. He's short.
10. They (feminine) are in the kitchen.

REVIEW EXERCISE 4

Complete each blank with the appropriate conjugated form of *ser* or *estar*.

1. *El carro* _____ *en el garaje,* _____ *un carro italiano. El carro* _____ *bonito pero* (but) _____ *muy caro* (expensive).

2. *¿Dónde* _____ *Carlos? Él* _____ *en la universidad. Carlos* _____ *un estudiante muy responsable* (responsible).

3. *Rosa y Felipe* _____ *en la playa. Ellos* _____ *turistas. Rosa* _____ *de México y Felipe* _____ *de Venezuela.*

4. *Nosotros* _____ *americanos. Ahora* _____ *en España con Ingrid y Sonia. Ingrid y Sonia* _____ *españolas.*

5. *Lucas* _____ *un estudiante muy responsable. Él siempre* (always) _____ *en la escuela pero hoy* (today) _____ *enfermo y* _____ *en la casa* (home).

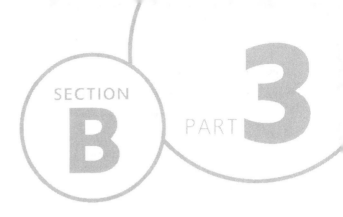

Answer Key

PRACTICE EXERCISE 1

1. preocupado – worried
2. enfermo – sick
3. cansado – tired
4. feliz – happy
5. triste – sad
6. confundido – confused
7. escuela – school
8. museo – museum
9. aeropuerto – airport
10. farmacia – pharmacy
11. hospital – hospital
12. playa – beach
13. pollo – chicken
14. cocina – kitchen
15. loco – crazy

PRACTICE EXERCISE 2

1. You would find many airplanes at an aeropuerto.
2. The room in the house where you're likely to make galletas is the cocina.
3. You buy your medicines in a farmacia.
4. She was triste before, but now she's feliz.
5. In the cocina you can make fried pollo.
6. She seems to be very confundida, she doesn't know what to do.
7. He was so enfermo that he was admitted in the hospital.
8. They have a wonderful Picasso in that museo.
9. In the summer, I like to spend the weekend in the playa.
10. He slept ten hours, he's no longer cansado.

PRACTICE EXERCISE 3

1. El farmacéutico está en la farmacia.
2. Los turistas están en el museo.
3. María y Ana están en el hospital.
4. Los gatos están en la sala.
5. Nosotros estamos en la universidad.
6. Tú y yo estamos en el cine.
7. Usted está en el teatro.
8. El señor está en el carro.
9. Ustedes están en el ferrocarril.
10. Pepa y tú están en la cocina.

PRACTICE EXERCISE 4

1. Nosotros estamos enfermos.
2. Yo estoy feliz.
3. Tú estás preocupado.
4. Clara y Jesús están tristes.

5. Enrique y Kevin están confundidos.
6. Juan y yo estamos cansados.
7. Ustedes están locos.
8. Usted está bien.
9. Ana María está feliz.
10. Las hormigas están confundidas.

REVIEW EXERCISE 1

1. Juan está triste.
2. Las manzanas son rojas.
3. Nosotros estamos en California.
4. Nosotros somos de California.
5. Cinco más uno es seis.
6. Yo estoy enfermo.
7. Ellas son inteligentes.
8. La mesa está en la cocina.
9. La mesa es italiana.
10. El café es colombiano.
11. ¡Hola! ¿Cómo estás?
12. Los taxis están ocupados.
13. Julia y Juan son altos.
14. Usted está feliz.
15. La muchacha es bonita.

REVIEW EXERCISE 2

1. Pedro es piloto. Él está en el aeropuerto.
2. Elena está en la escuela. Ella es estudiante.
3. Nosotros somos turistas. Nosotros estamos en el café.
4. Usted está en el hospital. Usted es doctor.
5. Silvia y Ricardo son actores. Ellos están en el teatro.

6. El señor Martínez está en la farmacia. Él es farmacéutico.
7. Rafael y Federico son aficionados. Ellos están en el concierto.
8. Ustedes son alpinistas. Ustedes están en la montaña.
9. Yo estoy en el parque. Yo soy turista.
10. Laura y Viviana son buenas bailarinas. Ellas están en la discoteca.

REVIEW EXERCISE 3

1. Yo estoy cansado/cansada, or Estoy cansado/cansada.
2. Nosotros somos estudiantes, or Somos estudiantes.
3. Ellos son de los Estados Unidos.
4. Ella es baja.
5. Usted está feliz.
6. Tú y yo somos escritores.
7. Usted es alto, or Vosotros/as sois altos/as.
8. Ustedes son dentistas.
9. Él es bajo.
10. Ellas están en la cocina.

REVIEW EXERCISE 4

1. El carro está en el garaje, es un carro italiano. El carro es bonito pero es muy caro.
2. ¿Dónde está Carlos? Él está en la universidad. Carlos es un estudiante muy responsable.
3. Rosa y Felipe están en la playa. Ellos son turistas. Rosa es de México y Felipe es de Venezuela.
4. Nosotros somos americanos. Ahora estamos en España con Ingrid y Sonia. Ingrid y Sonia son españolas.
5. Lucas es un estudiante muy responsable. Él siempre está en la escuela pero hoy está enfermo y está en la casa.

So, What's Next?
Taking Your Spanish Further

Now that you're off to a great start in Spanish, you probably want to build on what you've learned. There are many ways that you can take your Spanish further. If you're taking classes at school, well, keep doing that! And if you're not in school, there are probably courses that you can take in continuing education, at local community or cultural centers, or at private language schools. You could also practice what you know on the Internet or by listening to the radio or watching Spanish television. And maybe now you can use your Spanish to make a new friend!

No matter what you do, there are plenty of other fantastic Living Language® Spanish programs available that will help you get the most out of any class. Or, you can use them entirely on their own. Go to www.livinglanguage.com for a complete online catalogue with full descriptions. You'll also find a few highlighted programs on the following pages.

¡Buena suerte, y gracias!

Notes

Notes

_____

_____

_____

_____

_____

_____

_____

_____

_____

_____

_____

_____

_____

_____

_____

_____

_____

Notes

Notes

Notes

Notes

Notes